D1721521

RAVE REVIEWS FOR *MORE THAN A NOTION*

"Education systems are designed to replicate the societies that create them, and zip code is often determinative of student outcomes. In More Than A Notion, Dr. Tyrone Burton provides a path for school leaders to create schools, even Title I schools, designed overcome the many challenges that our students face. As a leader Dr. Burton led his school with passion and compassion and here he provides the blueprint for all school leaders to create schools where students can overcome the odds against them, and succeed."
–Nathan Dudley Ed.D., Field Support Liaison District 7,9,12
High Schools Bronx, NY

"As the superintendent of a school system where Dr. Burton led a school, I am very excited that he has written about the strategies and practices that lead to his success. In More Than A Notion, he provides a road map to the day to day work to accomplish the best outcomes for children. Serving today's children is a challenging task because of the multiple factors that must be addressed. This book does not just identify those factors, but more important, it identifies a plan of attack. Dr. Burton is an educator that has a greater passion and love for young people, this book clearly communicated just that!"
–T. Lamar Goree, Ph.D., Superintendent of
Caddo Parish Pubic Schools

"More than A Notion provides a reflective opportunity into the true nature of the principalship. The realities embedded allowed for veteran, as well as, new principals, to become successful as it relates to the varied responsibilities and sound deliverables. As a former principal and now a Superintendent, this book will be one I will use to develop principals and more importantly, provide credence to arguments affecting urban students."
–Gerald Fitzhugh, II, Ed.D., Superintendent of Schools,
Orange Township Public Schools

MORE THAN A
NOTION

A Journey in Educational
Leadership in the Age of Accountability

TYRONE D. BURTON, Ed.D.

Published by
Mynd Matters Publishing
715 Peachtree Street NE, Suites 100 & 200
Atlanta, GA 30308
www.myndmatterspublishing.com

978-1-948145-79-4 (Pbk)
978-1-948145-80-0 (hdcv)
978-1-948145-81-7 (eBook)
Library of Congress Control Number: 2020904635

FIRST EDITION

This book is dedicated to my mom, Claudette Calhoun Burton Jones, one of the most extraordinary women I have ever known.

On April 17, 2011, while attending the Induction Weekend Ceremony at Seton Hall University for Doctoral Students, my brother called to tell me our mom had died.

Having served as a first-grade teacher for twenty-nine and a half years, she was not just our mom, she was our first teacher. She instilled in us the idea that if our minds could conceive it and in our hearts, we believed it, we could achieve anything.

Therefore, her legacy of excellence, equity, and equality lives on in me. Because of her, I now realize that this great work is "More Than a Notion" but I stand ready for the call to action to serve this present age as my calling to fulfill.

CONTENTS

THE MATRIX OF LEADERSHIP IN THE AGE OF ACCOUNTABILITY

While serving as a principal, I had the opportunity to attend various workshops, classes, and professional development sessions; I also read a plethora of amazing books on leadership and the principalship. But none of them spoke comprehensively to my experience as a principal. I quickly realized that the principalship is "more than a notion." My mother would often use that phrase when she would talk to me about the vicissitudes of life. Leadership is not for the faint of heart.

Don't get me wrong: I am down with Dufour, fanatical about Fullan, and wild about Whitaker. I highly respect the work of scholars and professors. But there is a difference between the perspective of an academician and a practitioner. After successfully completing my dissertation at Seton Hall, I felt a burning desire to help other principals—hence the birth of this book.

I esteem the principalship as one of the most rewarding and challenging positions in the field of education. It is where the academic rubber meets the educational road of accountability. It is not for the faint of heart, or those who lack the desire to serve others through leading. Compared to other professions, it is one of the most difficult.

After attending undergraduate school and completing four (sometimes five) years of law school, lawyers finish with a Juris Doctorate and practice law. After eight years of school and a residency, physicians practice medicine. Most principals teach for five or seven years and complete a Master's of Education in Administration and Supervision, only to undertake one of the most difficult jobs in the country: creating productive citizens and lifelong learners. We don't get to practice the art of education; as we say in the South, we must "get 'er done," and our product is human capital.

In my opinion, all principals are like physicians (minus the salary and the fact that we don't get the luxury of practicing the art and science of education) for two distinct reasons:

1. They both treat or serve people. Doctors treat moms, dads, grandparents, boys, girls, teenagers, uncles, aunts, and transgender individuals. Principals will

primarily serve boys and girls; however, moms, dads, grandparents, aunts, and uncles are all stakeholders.

2. They both work in categories of service. The general practice physician will treat patients on a regular basis, but patients that need more specialized care will be referred to a specialist. For instance, when I went for a recent wellness exam, my physician referred me to a podiatrist and an optometrist, who referred me to an ophthalmologist.

Principals whose population mostly comes from middle-class and upper-class homes will generally have students who fit traditional parameters of a fundamental knowledge base, which is more akin to a general practitioner. For instance, these students will normally enter school knowing their names, their parents' names, and their address (or at least the name of their street). Most have seen and held a book, or have been read to. They might also know basic or primary colors and shapes.

If they come from a home where the average income is $150,000, they may have a functional vocabulary of 45 million words. If they come from a home where the average income is $50,000, they may have a functional vocabulary of 26 million words. Usually, they come from two-parent homes, and have been taught basic social skills (such as the difference between an inside and outside voice, or how to follow basic directions). Their parents also tend to be supportive of the school, and their parents and grandparents may have completed high school or college.

On the other hand, a Principal who serves under-resourced (academically and/or socially) students is more akin to a specialist. The traditional term for students in this category is "at risk," but I prefer to use the aforementioned term. Regardless of a child's socio-economic status, when they attended my school it was a safe zone, meaning that they were no longer at risk. When I use the term "under-resourced academically and/or socially," I mean that they may come from homes that fit the definition for generational or situational poverty as characterized by Ruby Payne in her book *Framework for Understanding Poverty*.[1] "Generational poverty" is defined as being in poverty two or more generations. "Situational poverty" is a shorter time and is caused by circumstances such as death divorce etc.

These students often come from households where the average income is less than $24,230, which is below the poverty line. Unlike students with upper-class or middle-class backgrounds, they may have a functional vocabulary of 13 million words. They are often very disorganized; for instance, they may lose papers or only complete part of an assignment. Students may also be physically aggressive, or like to entertain (Payne).[2]

The truth of the matter is that in this age of accountability, every principal will have to deal with the poverty gap, the hope gap, or both.

POVERTY GAP

According to the National Center for Children in Poverty, there are more than 72 million children under the age of eighteen in the United States. 32.4 million of these children live in low-income families, and 16.1 million children live in poor families.[3] These numbers have steadily increased: in 1989, 32% of all public-school children were from low-income families. In 2000, 38%; in 2006, 42%; in 2011, 48%; and by 2013, the rate "crossed the threshold of one half so that in 2013 low-income students became a new majority in the nation's public schools" (Southern Education Foundation).[4]

Flores (29) defines the poverty achievement gap as "a problem of unequal opportunities to learn experienced by many low-income students and many Latino and African American students." Flores found that poor students from these minority population centers "are less likely to have access to experienced and qualified teachers, more likely to face low expectations, and less likely to receive equitable per student funding" (30).[5]

According to Evans, Rothstein found that in virtually every place where these gaps have been studied, there is a strong correlation between students' literacy and the social elements of poverty. [6]

The Tauck Family Foundation, in collaboration with the Harvard Graduate School of Education, reported that the U.S. faces an education crisis that threatens the country's fiscal and social health: "Conquering the chronic achievement gap is considered both a moral imperative and pressing civil rights issue by many of our country's leaders, educators, and social entrepreneurs."[7] With the poverty achievement gap typically emerging at infancy, Tauck found that:

- Children from low-income households entering kindergarten and first grade were already significantly behind their more affluent peers in terms of academic knowledge, as well as cognitive and social skills.

- Third graders who both lived in poverty and read below grade level were three times more likely to drop out of high school than high income-level students.

- Fourth graders from low-income families were likely to be academically three years behind their peers from affluent families.

- Sixth graders in high-poverty schools who failed math, English, or received an unsatisfactory behavior grade had a 75% chance of dropping out of high school.

- Students in low-performing schools were five times

more likely to drop out of high school than their peers from high-performing schools. High school seniors from low-income families were, on average, four years behind their higher-income peers.

- One out of two students from low-income families graduated high school.
- 33% of high school students from low-income households went to college, and 8% completed a degree within six years of matriculation.

Tauck's findings confirm that the poverty achievement gap is one of the greatest challenges educators must face in the new age of high-stakes accountability.

Bogin and Nhuyen-Hoang[8] found that when Title I schools failed to meet adequate yearly progress for two years (and were therefore deemed failing), home values decreased—and further increased the stigma of living in high-need areas.

HOPE GAP

Jesse Jackson was correct when he said that we should keep hope alive. Amiri Baraka, who was once the principal of Central High School in Newark, New Jersey, has said that Central had such abysmal scores on the state proficiency exam given annually to juniors that it was in danger of being closed under the federal No Child Left Behind law.[9] With the help of a federal school improvement grant, he extended the school day, introduced small learning academics, integrated art and drama into academics, and hired consultants to coach teachers in literacy instruction. In addition to English and math, the test prep classes at Central High included a heavy dose of motivation. Teachers told students, "You can pass the test. You *must* pass it—for yourself, your school and your community."

When the scores were finally posted, seventy-two students had passed the math and literacy tests—more than a fivefold increase from the year before. In other words, he filled the hope gap.

I would like to close this section with a poem written by Tyler, a student at Central High.[10] His English teacher instructed students to respond to the word "hope:"

We hope to live
Live long enough to have kids
We hope to make it home every day
We hope we're not the next target to get sprayed...
We hope never to end up in Newark's dead pool
I hope, you hope, we all hope

I can recall my own efforts to fill the hope gap. In the morning, I would stand in front of the school, greet every student, and say, "Good morning. You look smart today."

During the morning announcements, we would recite the learner's creed:

I believe in myself to do my best and not waste this day.
I will listen.
I will think.
I will read.
I will write.
I will do all these things with one purpose in mind: to do my best and not waste this day, for this day will not come anymore.

The creed was followed by the pledge and the school's mission statement: "Members of the Cherokee Park Elementary community will function as a team to improve student achievement by providing high expectations for all stakeholders."

I was also very blessed to work with the best teachers in the district. We had teachers who routinely increased students' achievement levels by two years in one year, no matter what grade I placed them in. A few were able to accomplish this as soon as I hired them, but for the most part, I took the time to help them grow. We operated with big goals and expectations; now, many of them are principals, instructional coordinators, counselors, assistant principals, district supervisors, or educators at the state level.

I had to instill hope in them as they instilled hope in students. How does one instill hope in teachers who work with under-resourced students? I gave them space to vent, and I paid attention to the little things—birthdays, anniversaries, Girl Scout cookie sales. I was there for the big things, too. I'd visit them in the hospital and attend weddings and funerals. Most of all, I made sure they knew I was there to support them.

The challenge we face with under-resourced children may present itself as an achievement gap, but it really is a hope gap. Let me charge you to keep hope alive at your schools and school districts, because education is fundamentally a civil right.

Therefore, it is imperative principals and administrators who work with these students develop a skill set that will allow all stakeholders to succeed. You aren't just closing an achievement gap. You are closing a hope gap and giving opportunities for students.

The purpose of this book is to identify some of the struggles that are unique to principals who serve challenging populations. It also includes strategies that will increase your chances of instructional success—hence "The Matrix." The Matrix is composed of several awareness competences or skill sets I believe every school leader needs.

Chapters 1, 2 and 6 deal primarily with an awareness of systems and self, and delve into social and political awareness competences that are needed to be successful. Chapters 3, 4, and 5 deal primarily with skill sets that have been proven to be successful in schools where most students are under-resourced academically or socially. In Chapter 1, we will explore the historical context of the "haves and have nots" that permeate education, as well as the four frames of education that can counter systemic inequities. In Chapter 2, we will explore personality inventories of the principalship, and how to develop or maintain emotional intelligence. In Chapter 3, we will discuss how to develop a brand and message for your school. In Chapter 4, we will delve into the nitty and gritty of leading beyond the turnaround process. In Chapter 5, we will discuss student achievement, and determine whether educators should be data-driven or data-informed. In Chapter 6, we will reflect on how to navigate the vicissitudes of the principalship. Chapter 7 is a call to action.

I will also refer to the spiritual dimensions of leadership. At times, I may sound a little preachy—but it is just my passion flowing through. Ultimately, I hope that this book helps you be a better educator!

THE ERA / ERROR OF ACCOUNTABILITY

In his article, "A Nation of 'Haves' and 'Have Nots?'", Tom Rosentiel makes the claim that there are indeed two systems of education in America.[11] As an educator, I am painfully aware of this inequity; even so, the first time I read D'Amico's statement was like a slap of reality. From that moment on, all of my educational decisions were intentionally focused on repairing the breach between the haves and have nots. In other words, I stopped drinking the proverbial Kool-Aid®.

All of your decisions must be based on what is best for your students, whether you are a principal or a superintendent. It sounds cliché, but far too often we simply do what we are told. Contrary to popular belief, size does matter—and one size doesn't fit or fix every problem. Doing the correct thing may not always be the right thing. In order to do the right thing, you must equip yourself with a complete understanding of the system and be pedagogically sound.

For instance, our accountability system has nothing to do with systemic equity, equality, education, or accountability. Nowhere in our profession is inequity and inequality so profound as it is when it comes to accountability (i.e., state tests). Education is a civil right that has been distorted by the notion of closing the achievement gap. We should closing be the hope gap. But before we discuss the error of accountability caused by the Every Student Succeeds Act (ESSA), No Child Left Behind (NCLB), the National Governors Association (NGA), and the Council of Chief State School Officers (CCSSO), we need to briefly examine another era and the Eight-Year Study.

THE ERA

In this study, thirty schools were promised that approximately 300 colleges would drop traditional entrance requirements if they could thoroughly demonstrate that their students were prepared for college.[12] The thirty schools were free to experiment with their curriculums, because they were not constrained by the universal standards for college admissions. One aim of the study was to test, on a national scale, how the progressive/experimentalist philosophy affected cognitive, social, and emotional growth. This was the height of the progressive movement in American education.

Schools were free to develop their curricular programs to meet the needs of their students and stakeholders. Teachers, administrators, and university professors worked together to develop problem-based programs. The evaluation of the study used a matched-pairs design and tracked students through college (meaning there were approximately 2,400 students in the experimental group, and 2,400 similar students in the control group). The study revealed there is no set standard that best prepares students for college. Students from the experimental schools did better academically in college than their peers from traditional high schools. In fact, they found these students:

- earned a higher total grade average
- earned higher grade averages in all subjects except foreign language
- specialized in the same academic fields as the comparison students
- were not placed on academic probation at higher rates than the comparison group
- received more academic honors each year
- operationalized the Cardinal Principles of Secondary Education of 1918 in thirty different high school systems across the country (health, command of fundamental processes, worthy home membership, vocation, citizenship, worthy use of leisure, and ethical character)

- possessed a high degree of intellectual curiosity and drive
- were more precise, systematic, and objective in their thinking
- earned a higher percentage of non-academic honors in college
- developed clear or well-formulated ideas concerning the meaning of education, especially in the first two years of college
- demonstrated a high degree of resourcefulness in new situations
- did not differ from the comparison group in their ability to plan their time effectively
- had similar problems as the comparison group, but their solutions were more effective
- demonstrated a more active concern regarding current events

To put it more succinctly, they were taught to engage in critical thinking and problem-solving, and developed a sense of global integrity and responsibility.

Now that we have established that standardization is not the best route to create lifelong learners, let's look at our current system. If standardization is not the best route, why are we implementing it in our schools?

THE ERROR

Before I dive deep into the abyss of systemic national standardization, let me emphasize that I believe the National Assessment of Educational Progress (NAEP), Programme for International Student Assessment (PISA), and Trends in International Mathematics and Science Study (TIMMS) have a rightful place in education. My bias is that I am an educational centralist and progressivist. I believe that curriculum needs to be developed at the local level, allowing administrators and teachers to use methods such as problem-based, project-based, and inquiry-based learning in order to teach students how to think critically and solve problems.

The Obama administration advocated for education standards that prepared high school graduates for college and a career. To achieve this, the administration pressured states to adopt content standards known as the Common Core, which was developed by the National Governors Association and the Council of Chief State School Officers (NGA/CCSSO). The administration also called for federal Title I aid to be withheld from states that did not adopt Common Core or comparable standards. The NGA/CCSSO standards development process was quickly completed by Achieve, Inc., a private contractor. Research also indicates that the level of input from school-based practitioners was minimal, and the standards had not been field-tested. It is also unclear whether the tests used to measure the academic outcomes will be able to justify the high-stakes consequences. William J. Mathis's research at the University of Colorado Boulder suggests that schools with high academic standards fare no better (or worse) than those with low academic standards.[13] Research for standards–driven, test-based accountability systems is similarly weak. Additionally, nations with centralized standards perform no better or worse on inter-national tests than those without centralized standards.

Mathis made the following recommendations based on his research:

- The NGA/CCSSO Common Core standards initiative should be continued, but only as a low-stakes advisory and assistance tool for curriculum improvement, articulation, and professional development.

- The NGA/CCSSO Common Core standards should be subjected to extensive trials and subsequent revision before implementation. During this time, states should be encouraged to carefully examine and experiment with broad-based school evaluation systems.

- Given the strengths and weaknesses of testing, policymakers should not implement high-stakes accountability systems where the assessments are inadequate for such purposes. [14]

Unfortunately, his recommendations were ignored—hence NCLB, CCSS, and its latest version, the Every Student Succeeds Act (ESSA).

The Every Student Succeeds Act was signed into law on December 10, 2015, and put an end to the No Child Left Behind Act—an onerous federal policy that has dogged schools for over a decade. ESSA is the most recent version of the federal government's comprehensive K-12 law, the Elementary and Secondary Education Act (ESEA), which went into effect in 1965 (and we all know things were going just great educationally in 1965, huh?). ESSA passed in December 2015 with broad bipartisan support and reauthorized the Elementary and Secondary Education Act of 1965 as amended. The ESEA initially offered grants to districts serving low-income students, federal grants for textbooks and library books, and scholarships for low-income college students. Additionally, the law provided federal grants to state educational agencies (SEAs) in order to improve the quality of elementary and secondary education. The ESEA has been periodically reauthorized by Congress, with the version prior to ESSA being the No Child Left Behind Act of 2001 (NCLB). The rewrite of the law was accomplished through a bipartisan legislative process—a process that has been increasingly rare in Washington. Herein lies the problem—the same political machine that authorized NCLB put ESSA in place. The law was passed in 2015. In 2017, states drafted their plans, which included: new accountability systems; needs assessments for struggling schools; strategies for targeting federal funding; implementing programs; and monitoring their progress with educators. This means we still have accountability, but instead of having one national accountability system, each state decides how accountability is measured. The extremely sad thing is the more things change, the more they stay the same.

THE ESSA-NCLB CONNECTION

To make it plain, ESSA is built on the foundational premise of NCLB. And as I mentioned earlier, NCLB was supposedly a reauthorization of the Elementary and Secondary Education Act of 1965. Now, let's take a deeper look at NCLB and the fallacies it was built upon.

Regarding NCLB, former U.S. Secretary of Education Rod Paige said, "America's children depend on us. We must not thrust that burden onto our posterity. It is ours to bear." In 2001, President George W. Bush said, "Good education starts in the living rooms of the citizens of this country. It starts with a mom or a dad saying, 'You turn off the TV and practice reading.' It means, get rid of the tube and get into the books."[15]

In 2001, NCLB was enacted in order to usher in a new era of education. It was not sold as a Republican law or a

Democratic law, but an American law. In August of that same year, President George W. Bush boldly said, "When it comes to the education of our children…failure is not an option."[16] I was assigned my first principalship in 2001, and let me tell you, a lot of children were left behind after the implementation of this law. As Albert Einstein brilliantly said, "Insanity: the belief that one can get different results by doing the same thing." At its best, NCLB was a well-intended underfunded law. It offered four reform principles:

- Accountability: Guaranteeing Results
- Flexibility: Local Control for Local Challenges
- Research-Based Reforms: Proven Methods with Proven Results
- Parental Options: Choices for Parents, Hope for Kids[17]

In fact, a staple of the law was that accountability began with informed parents, communities, and elected leaders. The law measured progress by testing every child in grades three through eight in math and reading. States would also implement fair and effective annual tests, which would be funded by the government. If schools didn`t improve, NCLB guaranteed that:

- Parents, voters and taxpayers would know if schools are improving.
- States would implement fair and effective annual tests.

- Washington would provide funding to states to design and implement tests.

Because of NCLB, we received school report cards and funding based on scores that we wouldn't see until the following school year. More funding was given to safe and drug-free school zones during this period of educational enlightenment as well. Fast forward to President Barack Obama, who more adequately funded the law—hence Common Core.

THE PROBLEM(S) WITH COMMON CORE

Let's review the genesis of Common Core. On June 1, 2009, the National Governors Association Center for Best Practices (NGA) and the Council of Chief State School Officers (CCSSO) announced that forty-six states, the District of Columbia, and two U.S. territories had agreed to join the Common Core Standards Initiative and develop common standards for math and language arts.

Over 170 organizations pledged their support for the initiative. Yet the evidence presented by the NGA and CCSSO was lacking compared to independent reviews. Research suggested the CCSS and those who supported them were misguided. The standards had not been validated empirically, and no metric monitored the consequences of Common Core (Mathis).[18] Support of the CCSS collapses under a review of empirical literature: a) America's children are lagging‖ behind international peers in terms of academic achievement, and b) the economic vibrancy and future of the United States relies upon students outranking their global peers on international tests of academic achievement because of the mythical relationship between test scores and a country's economic competitiveness (Tienken; Canton; Zhao).[19]

It seems as though those who penned their support for the CCSS did not read the evidence refuting their argument, or else they did not understand it. The contention that a test result can influence the future economic prowess of a country like the United States or any of the G20 nations represents an unbelievable suspension of logic. To believe otherwise is like believing in the tooth fairy. The U.S. already has one of the highest percentages of people with high school diplomas and college degrees, and we had the greatest number of 15-year-old students score the highest levels on the 2006 PISA science test (OECD; United Nations).[20]

We produce more researchers, scientists, and qualified engineers than our economy can employ, and we are one of the most economically competitive nations in the globe (Gereffi and Wadhwa 2005; Lowell et al., 2009; Council on Competitiveness, 2011; World Economic Forum, 2011).[21] When trying to extricate the facts from fiction, it is important to understand that not all economies are created equal (Baker; Rameriz, Luo, Schofer, and Meyer;

Tienken).[22] Nations with strong economies (e.g., the G20) demonstrate a weaker relationship between educational attainment (e.g., output on international tests, percentage of population with at least a BA degree) and economic growth. Japan is an example of this phenomenon. Japan's stock market, the Nikkei 225 Average, closed at a high of 38,915 points on December 31, 1989. On October 15, 2010, it closed at 9,500 points, approximately 75% lower. However, Japan has been in the Top 10 on international math tests since the 1980s, and has always ranked higher than the U.S. Yet Japan's stock market and its economy have been in shambles for almost two decades. Japan has had national curriculum standards and testing for over thirty years. Japanese students outrank students from most other nations on math and science tests.

In contrast, the Dow Jones Industrial Average broke 1,200 points for the first time on April 26, 1983, the day "A Nation at Risk" by the National Commission on Excellence in Education was released. The Dow closed at 11,691 points on January 4, 2011—over a ten-fold increase. The U.S. consistently outranks Japan on the World Economic Forum's Growth Competitiveness Index. Since 1984, the GDPs of Japan and the U.S. have essentially grown at the same rates. The U.S. posted a third-quarter GDP in 2010 that was approximately 3.74 times larger than in 1984, whereas Japan's 2010 third-quarter GDP was 3.48 times larger than in 1984 (advantage U.S., regardless of what some call poor international test rankings). The U.S. had approximately twice the number of 15-year-old students who scored at the top levels of the 2006 PISA science test compared to Japan. The U.S. also accounted for 25% of the top-scoring students in the world on that test, even though the U.S. did not outrank Japan overall.

In the G20 nations, the education system needs the economy more than the economy needs the education system. Competitive, nimble, and expanding labor markets in countries with strong economies drive citizens to seek higher levels of education. This was recognized over 50 years ago when Harbison and Myers noted, "Education is both the seed and flower of economic development."[23] The U.S. has been ranked first or second in the World Economic Forum's Global Competitiveness Index (GCI) for eight years, and has never ranked below sixth place throughout the last ten years—regardless of results on international assessments and or national curriculum standards.

No other country has ranked more consistently on the GCI. The U.S. workforce is one of the most productive and best-educated in the world. In 2009, over 70% of recent high school graduates were enrolled in college (Bureau of Labor Statistics).[24] Approximately 30% of U.S. adults between the ages twenty-five and thirty-four have at least a bachelor's degree. Six other industrialized nations have a higher percentage of adults with a bachelor's degree (OECD)[25] but their economies pale in comparison.

The U.S. leads the world in utility patents, or patents for innovations. In 2009, the U.S. was granted 95,037 patents, whereas Japan, the country with the next greatest number of patents, was granted 38,006.[26]

The other countries of the world combined were only granted 96,896 patents (U.S. Patent and Trademark Office).[27] The U.S is home to over 28% of the patents granted globally, which is the largest percentage of any country. Japan is second with 20%. The U.S. is second to Japan for the number of Trademarks—1.7 million versus 1.4 million. (World Intellectual Property Organization).[28]

According to the World Economic Forum, the U.S. has an outstanding university system.[29] It is home to eleven out of the top fifteen universities in the world; the United Kingdom is next, with three out of the fifteen. It seems illogical that the country with the best university system in the world can have a failing PK-12 education system that needs to be placed under centralized curricular control.

McCluskey reported that out of twenty-seven nations that outranked the U.S. on the 2006 PISA science test, ten of those nations did not have national standards, whereas twelve of the twenty-eight nations that ranked lower than the U.S. had national standards. The same pattern held true for the 2007 Grade 8 TIMSS mathematics results. Although the eight countries that outranked the U.S. on that test had national standards, so did thirty-three of the thirty-nine countries that ranked lower. The students from nations with national standards ranked lower than the U.S. students. The TIMSS science assessment had similar results.[30]

Tienken found no statistically significant relationship between the top twenty-two performing economies in the world and their ranks on international math and science tests.[31] Salzman and Lowell confirmed that 90% of the variance in PISA test scores is explained by factors within countries, not between countries.[32] Why do we focus on a solution that, at best, will provide a 10% improvement? The evidence offered by the NGA and CCSSO is nothing more than snake oil. This is not data-driven decision making. This is a decision grasping for data.

Perhaps there is another explanation for scoring high on international tests. I noticed that all twenty-four industrialized countries that outscored the U.S. on the 2006 PISA mathematics test has some form of universal healthcare system, whereas the U.S. and 40% of the countries that scored lower than U.S. students do not (World Health Organization).[33] Most of the countries that outscored the U.S. also have lower child mortality rates, and most have longer overall life expectancies (CIA).[34] Only Poland, Slovakia, and Hungary have shorter life expectancies and still outscore the U.S. on international tests. Many of the countries that outscore the U.S. also have comprehensive fair housing policies.

Housing policy has been shown to be a stronger intervention for high test scores than nationalizing curriculum (Schwartz).[35] Perhaps it's not universal curriculum standards that make the difference. Maybe it's a comprehensive social system. The data points in that direction. Although this would not qualify as an empirical argument, it does highlight some interesting relationships and is just as strong as the evidence offered to support nationalized standards—maybe stronger.

The vendors of the CCSS claim that the standards address critical skills necessary to compete in the twenty-first century. If so, why do they repackage nineteenth century ideas? We only need to look at the mid-1800s and the Lancasterian method (used in London and some of America's cities, including Quincy, Massachusetts) to see how the idea of standardization will play out. It did not work then, and it will not work now.

SOLUTIONS, ANYONE?

So, what does the research suggest in terms of centralized curriculum planning? Wang, Haertel, and Walberg found that curriculum has the greatest influence on student achievement when it is a proximal variable in the education process. They found that the closer to the student that the curriculum is designed, deliberated, and created, the greater influence it has on learning.[36]

This means a curriculum should largely be a local endeavor. When a curriculum is treated as something that is handed down from on high, as is the case with the CCSS, it has a much weaker influence.

National policy mandates have the weakest influence of all on student learning; like the CCSS, they are distal to the actual learning process.[37]

Tramaglini found similar results while studying the 120 New Jersey high schools that serve the state's poorest communities. Tramaglini found that the more proximal the curriculum development process, the better the students performed on the state's high school exit exam.[38] Reed reported that universal curriculum standards do not close the achievement gap.[39] The achievement gap is not a product of an expectations gap, and local school contexts explain more of the achievement gap than universal standards.

In another 2002 study of course-taking before and after the introduction of New York's regent standards revealed that local contexts, such as school size and demographics, accounted for most of the disparity in course-taking. Universal curriculum requirements did little to overcome that after their initial implementation. Local context, involvement, and input matters greatly.

But we have studies from others as well. The landmark

Eight-Year Study demonstrated that a curriculum can be an entirely locally-developed project and still produce better results than traditional curricular programs (Aikin).[40] In fact, the experiment demonstrated that the less standardized the programs, the better the students did in college academically, socially, and civically compared their traditionally prepared peers. Results from several well-known earlier studies demonstrated that there is not one best curriculum path for students in high school, and standardized curricula sequences are not necessary to achieve superior results. (Collings and Kilpatrick; Jersild, Thorndike, Goldman, Wrightstone and Loftus; Thorndike; Wrightstone, Rechetnick, McCall, and Loftus; Wrightstone 1936).[41]

Equality of curriculum standards is inherently inequitable. Mandating that students follow the same set of standards and perform at the same level of achievement guarantees that certain groups of students will lose.

There is no reliable, independently validated empirical support for the CCSS initiative, and yet many policy-makers and educators support it. It is an attractive idea because it limits the intricacies of the real issues and makes it easy to blame a system (public education) that reacts to society, not drives it. The CCSS initiative compartmentalizes complexity, and compartmentalizing messy issues allows people to be intellectually lazy. Developing coherent education and social policy is more difficult. The vendors of the CCSS present standardization as a neat and clean solution, manageable and easy to discuss. Unfortunately, the real world is not so organized, and it is much more cognitively complicated. Believing that we can eliminate the complexity of education by implementing one-size-fits-all standards is like believing rankings on international tests mean something. (Is your tooth under the pillow?)

The evidence suggests that there is not a crisis in education; there is a crisis in education leadership. Those who perpetuate bad ideas based on flawed data are practicing poor leadership. If they do not want to stand up for children, then they should sit down and let others take the reins.

School leaders do not have to conduct research on these topics, but they should at least dig below the surface of relevant research. Children have a right to a quality education. School leaders, those who prepare them, and the people who lead our professional organizations have a duty to help provide it. Children do not have a seat at the policy-making table. Policy is thrust upon them, not created with them. They are helpless to defend themselves against poor decision making.

THE FOUR FRAMES OF EDUCATION

The most important tools we have as educational leaders are the four frames of education. In times of stress, people tend fault each other, blame the bureaucracy, complain about their powerlessness, or become an organizational drone (rather than take responsibility and lead others to a preferred future). This is why awareness and the implementation of Boleman and Deal's research is so important.[42] The frames provide a way to think through multiple perspectives:

- Symbolic (temple)—meaning, purpose
- Human Resource (family)—people, group dynamics
- Structural (factory)—process, task-based
- Political (jungle)—resources, social influence, control, negotiating, power

Knowing how to effectively navigate between the frames is one of the keys to great leadership. Organizations are living systems that are in a constant state of flux, much like the human body. It changes daily and adjusts based on the brain's commands. As the leader, you must be the brain and utilize the four frames to keep the organization thriving.

The Structural Frame deals primarily with how organizations or systems operate. This is mostly done by defining clear roles, rules, goals, policies, technologies, and environmental expectations. The challenge of implementing this frame is properly aligning people, processes, and technology to enhance the structure, as well as being constantly attuned to its needs. Remember that every organization is perfectly aligned for the results that it gets. Principals must be constantly aware of resource alignment.

Some guiding questions you should ask as you implement this frame are:

- Do I have the right people in the right places doing the right things?
- Are the organization's policies clear, and are the rules aligned to implement these policies?
- Are the goals in the organization doable and sustainable?
- Will the technology that we are currently using inhibit or enhance the structure?
- Are the expectations for the environment clear, and am I modeling them?

Answering these questions could lead to some uncomfortable conversations, but it will help the organization run more smoothly.

The Human Resources Frame deals primarily with how you interact with people in the organization. More specifically, it addresses relationships, self-interest, needs, feelings, and skills. The challenge in this frame is being attuned to human needs without sacrificing the goals of the organization. This is done by taking time to build trust and confidence as a leader. Every organization is perfectly aligned for the trust that you give. Key concepts to keep in mind as you implement this frame are:

- You must be the change that you want to see in others.

- Ronald A. Heifetz and Donald L. Laurie claimed that leaders must create and maintain an organizational environment in which people can transform stress into work.[43] A certain level of tension is necessary to mobilize people, but leaders must find a balance between how much pressure individuals can tolerate and how much pressure they need in order to adapt.

Learning how to navigate this frame will pay great dividends for you and the organization.

The Political Frame deals primarily with power, politics, self-interest, competition, conflicts, and intrigue. The challenges of this frame are developing an agenda, forming coalitions to build a solid power base, acquiring good intelligence, and learning how to dispense information wisely. Many principals shy away from this frame because they feel that politics is for politicians, but the truth is politics is an important prominent part of our business (NCLB, CCSSO, NGA, etc.). We must embrace it and make it a part of our skill set. Some key concepts in this frame are:

- forming partnerships with local businesses, not just to solicit their support, but make them aware of the school's progress
- developing a professional relationship with your school board members and keeping them updated on

the school's needs
- welcoming local teacher organizations so they can serve their constituents
- attending community board meetings and advocating for your school to alleviate any false perceptions
- joining professional organizations and becoming active in their endeavors

People's perception is most often based on the media or what they hear from people of influence. Politics and power are influential. Therefore, you must become involved in your community so you can shape their perception.

Finally, there is the Symbolic Frame, which is probably one of the most powerful frames. When used correctly, it inspires people to have hope. For instance, the United States is a symbol. Each state has a flag as a symbol. On the top of most churches is a cross, which is a symbol. Commercial products that are sold all have symbols, such as the golden arches of McDonalds. Symbols evoke passion and speak volumes even when mouths are closed.

The key concepts in this frame are:
- ritual
- ceremony
- metaphors
- meaning
- stories

- culture
- heroes and heroines
- common good

Symbols inspire, create faith, define beauty, and identify meaning. I believe schools are the best places to incorporate this frame.

For instance, our school had several rituals, such as reciting the pledge, learner's creed, and mission statement every morning. We had a theme every year and matching T-shirts to wear on designated days.

We also used an event (Symbolic) to utilize all four frames and solve a schoolwide problem (Structural). The goal was to decrease the referral rate to the office (Structural), increase school pride (Humanistic), and involve the community (Political).

Our average mobility rate was approximately 36%, which is especially high for an elementary school. This meant that we had a constant flow of new students, and we had to help them acclimate to our school culture and climate. During one faculty meeting, the entire staff (Political/Humanistic) looked at the referral data and discussed which school rules (Structural) were violated the most. We came up with ten essential rules (Structural) that we felt were necessary for all students and would enhance our school climate (Humanistic). Hence, Tribal Council was born (Symbolic, Political, Structural, and Humanistic). It was loosely based on Ron Clark Academy's House Wars.

I know you are wondering how we used one event to incorporate all frames. The first thing we did was decide the criteria for our Tribal Council (Structural). We created a rubric and assigned points to each area of focus. We posted the ten rules in conspicuous places throughout the school (Symbolic). One of our teachers wrote a song using the ten rules, which we made into an infomercial starring students and staff (Political/Humanistic). The video was played at our annual Back to School Bash, so parents and community partners knew what we were doing (Political).

Our school was divided into tribes. Each tribe had the liberty of choosing its own name, symbol, colors, and chant (Symbolic/Humanistic). They were as follows:

Tribe	Symbol	Color
Seneca (Pre-K – K)	Lion	Purple
Apache (1st – 2nd)	Sun	Yellow
Caddo (3rd – 4th)	Eagles	Orange
Mohican (5th – 6th)	Wolves	Black

Once a month we had Tribal Council (Structural), which included the following:

- a press release (Political)
- rules for the competition, such as practice times, academic focus, time allotted to display their talent,

where to sit in the auditorium, and how to enter the auditorium (Structural)

- six external judges—such as central office staff, local political leaders, radio and TV personalities, other principals, retired administrators, and our business partner—to score the competition using the rubric (Political)

The judges were advised to arrive to school thirty minutes before the Tribal Council began so that our teacher Spirit Leader (Humanistic) and conductor of the Tribal Council could go over the rubric with them (Structural). When the judges arrived, we would give them a branded water bottle, a light snack, a personalized name tag, and a folder with all the information in it (Symbolic, Humanistic, Structural, and Political). Then, we would have an announcer read the biography of each judge as they entered the auditorium (Humanistic/Symbolic). We had an agenda (Structural/Political) and gave a trophy to the winning tribe at the end of competition (Symbolic).

Our average attendance rate was around 96%, which indicated that our students loved coming to school. Office referrals also decreased. This had a profoundly positive impact on our school, and school events would not even have standing room. The community fully supported the school, which increased school pride.

FINDING AND REFINING EFFECTIVE LEADERSHIP

The two most important days in your life
is the day when you were born and the
day you find out why.
—Mark Twain

If leading is not your passion, then you are in the wrong position. King David, one of my favorite Biblical writers, said, "For as a man thinks in his heart, so is he" (Proverbs 23:7, New King James Version). Steven Covey said, "Seek first to understand and then be understood."[44] *Meditations in Wall Street* says, "What lies behind us and what lies before us a small matter compared to what lies within us."[45] Who are you, really? You know your name, where you were born, and who your parents are—but at your core, who are you? What makes you gravitate to some people and shy away from others? Or are you more comfortable by yourself? More succinctly, why do you do the things you do?

Minister Ernest T. Campbell was speaking from a real place of life centeredness when he said, "The two most important days in your life is the day when you were born and the day you find out why."[46] I believe life centeredness is the place where purpose and passion meet. You cannot find, ignite, or reignite your passion until you know your purpose. People who live passion-filled lives truly know their purpose.

Here are a few examples that demonstrate a life centeredness point of view. The passion of Jesus dying on the cross was evident in His purpose-driven life because He would say things like, "I am the way the truth and the life," (John 14:6, New International Version), or "For I have come down from heaven not to do my will but to do the will of him who sent me. " (John 6: 38, NIV).

Martin Luther King Jr. spoke from a place of passion at the March on Washington in 1963 when he said, "I have a dream deeply rooted in the American dream...that one day this nation will rise up, and live out the true meaning of its creed."[47] He prefaced it by stating that he knew there were some difficult days ahead. He could speak so vehemently because he spoke from a place of life centeredness and passion.

Mastermind Bill Gates is quoted as saying, "Don`t

compare yourself to anyone in this world… if you do so, you are insulting yourself." [48] He also said, "[Intelligence is] an elusive concept. There's a certain sharpness, an ability to absorb new facts. To walk into a situation, have something explained to you and immediately say, 'Well, what about this?' To ask an insightful question. To absorb it in real time. A capacity to remember. To relate to domains that may not seem connected at first. A certain creativity that allows people to be effective." He could convey such thoughts because he was following his passion—one that the world had yet to imagine.

Your Purpose + Passion = Life Centeredness

Purpose and passion are like grace and mercy—you can`t have one without the other. The combined experience results in life centeredness. I believe people who know their purpose and follow their passion are often transformational leaders. I will talk more about that later, but I will use the terms passion-driven and transformational synonymously.

The entire process of achieving life centeredness begins with the process of self-actualization. In other words, you can`t grow until you know yourself. Your position does not define who you are. It may dictate what you do professionally, but it doesn't define who you are. Simply being a principal, pastor, or CEO does not—and should not—define who you are as a person, but far too often it does. Far too often we develop habits in order to fit our image. Professional literature is replete with examples and definitions of leadership, making it easy for a true seeker of self-actualization to get lost. Sometimes it is easier for us to describe passionate leadership, as opposed to defining and developing it.

In this chapter, we will discuss three different personality inventories, as well as emotional intelligence. Knowing who you are as a leader involves a lot of reflection and exploration into your emotional landscape and personality styles. The objective of this chapter is for leaders to learn their temperaments, personalities, and tendencies, as well as how they can maximize their ability to grow themselves and others on their leadership team. The question posed in this chapter is, *who are you?*

Personality is another component of who we are as leaders, and it is something to understand rather than to develop. In contrast, recent research suggests that we can develop emotional intelligence. An awareness of your unique personality will give you insight into what you feel, how you respond, and how to manage your emotions (as well as the emotions of others).

Personality is an individual's patterned body of habits, traits, attitudes, and thoughts. Personality traits include tendencies towards introversion or extroversion, how you get your energy, how you process information, and approaches to decision-making (Aguilar).[49]

Understanding your personality will enable you play to your strengths, accept yourself, and identify areas of growth. Understanding your own personality boosts the self-awareness component of your emotional intelligence, and understanding the personalities of your leadership team boosts their social awareness and social management (Aguilar).[50]

Most companies use one of three personality inventories to help their employees better understand themselves and each other. These personality inventories are True Colors, the Keirsey Temperament Sorter, and the Psycho-Geometric System, all of which are research-based methods with merit. However, I suggest that passion-driven leaders take all three personality inventories in conjunction with fully understanding their emotional intelligence. If you go to your doctor for a routine physical, they are going to administer several tests in order to have a complete picture of your health. Why not do the same when working with people? Remember, you can't grow yourself until you know yourself. You can't build capacity in your organization until you know what makes you tick. People tend to follow and respect leaders who know how to build bridges of trust. Trust is the feeling of confidence we have in another's character and competence (Covey).[51] And to cultivate trust, we need to know ourselves as leaders (Coaching).[52] Self-knowledge is the foundation upon which trust is established. According to Michael Fullan, cultivating trust might be the hardest thing about building teams.[53] Let's go a little deeper and examine some personality inventories.

The first one we will examine is the Psycho-Geometric inventory, created by Susan E. Dellinger, Ph.D.[54] Dr. Dellinger created this system in 1978 as a solution to a problem. When she was the management trainer for a Fortune 50 corporation, she became frustrated with the cumbersome and complicated personality tests and decided to create something better. While working on her doctorate in communication at the University of Colorado, she developed a communication-style analysis based on five simple geometric shapes. The pros to using this system is that it is quick, easy to understand and equally as valid as other test on the market. The shapes are square, triangle, rectangle, circle, and squiggle. People who choose square, triangle, or rectangle tend to be left-brain thinkers, taking a logical and organized approach to life. People who choose circle or squiggle tend to be right-brain thinkers. They tend to process information in a less linear way. They are more interested in the whole rather than its individual parts, and emphasize creativity and intuition.

The second inventory we will examine is the Keirsey Temperament Sorter. David Keirsey expanded on Hippocrates and Plato's study of temperament.[55] It is a self-assessed personality questionnaire designed to help people better understand themselves and others. Although the questionnaire can take a long time to finish, it is one of the most widely used personality assessments in the world. Its user base consists of major employers like Bank of America, Allstate, the U.S. Air Force, and IBM. Keirsey used the names suggested by Plato: Artisan, Guardian, Idealist, and Rationalist. People who are Artisans are concrete and adaptable. They are concerned with making an impact, and their greatest strength is tactics. They excel in troubleshooting, agility, and manipulation of tools and equipment. They tend to be operators and entertainers.

Guardians are concrete and organized. They are concerned with responsibility and duty, and their greatest strength is logistics. They excel at organizing, facilitating, and supporting. They tend to be administrators and conservators.

Idealists are abstract and compassionate. They are concerned with personal growth and finding their own identity. Their greatest strength is diplomacy, and they excel at clarifying, individualizing, unifying, and inspiring. They tend to be mentors and advocates.

Rationalists are abstract and objective. They are concerned with their own knowledge and competence. Their greatest strength is strategy, and they excel in any kind of logical investigation. They tend to be coordinators and engineers.

The third and final assessment we will examine is True Colors. Don Lowry developed True Colors, which uses four primary colors to designate personality types and behavioral styles.[56] It was designed to maximize the application of psychological style in different communities, and he hoped it would result in positive self-worth and self-esteem. Dowry also believed that with increased understanding of ourselves and others, conflict will decrease. Each color is associated with certain personality traits or behaviors. Everyone has some degree of each color, but one color is dominant. This inventory is not as lengthy as the Keirsey inventory, but it is lengthier than the Dellinger inventory. The colors are orange, gold, green, and blue.

People whose predominate color is orange tend to act on a moment's notice. They are witty, charming, spontaneous, impulsive, generous, impactful, optimistic, eager, and bold. They value skill, resourcefulness, and courage. They are natural troubleshooters.

People whose predominate color is gold tend to follow rules and respect authority. They are loyal, dependable, prepared, thorough, sensible, punctual, faithful, stable, caring, and concrete. They value home, family, and tradition. They are also natural helpers.

People whose predominate color is green tend to seek knowledge and understanding. They are analytical, global, conceptual, cool, calm, collected, inventive, logical, perfectionist, abstract, and investigative. They value intelligence, insight, and fairness, and are non-conformist visionaries.

People whose predominate color is Blue tend to feel unique and authentic. They are enthusiastic, sympathetic, personal, warm, communicative, compassionate, idealist, spiritual, sincere, peaceful, and imaginative. They value integrity, unity in relationships, and are natural romantics and nurturers.

A completed personality profile may look like this: squiggle, gold, ESTJ. Remember, you can't grow yourself until you know yourself. As a leader, you may choose to only give one of the three assessments to your team; however, I would suggest that those closest to you take the entire battery of assessments. The last piece of the self-actualization puzzle deals with your emotional intelligence. If you are emotionally aware, you won't suffer quite as much when people make withdrawals from your emotional bank. Emotional Intelligence (EI) is simply the knowledge we have about our feelings. Emotions—positive and negative—are contagious. Therefore, it is imperative you can manage yours, as well the emotions of your leadership team. Passion-driven leadership requires emotionally stable leaders. You must be the anchor that holds the ship in place when the emotional waters get rough. Passion-driven leaders are the bedrock of solace when the vicissitudes of life come to work.

Travis Bradberry, co-author of *Emotional Intelligence 2.0* and co-founder of TalentSmart, conducted research which indicates that emotional intelligence is responsible for 58% of job performance.[57] Those who lack emotional intelligence are at a significant disadvantage. His research further suggests that there are nine types of people who never succeed at work, because their lack of emotional intelligence harms their careers and others. They are as follows:

The Coward

Cowardly colleagues are quick to blame others and to cover up important mistakes. They usually fail to stand up for what is right. Fear is an extremely powerful motivator.

The Dementor

Dementors suck the life out of the room by imposing their negativity upon everyone they encounter. Their viewpoints are always glass half empty, and they can inject fear and concern into even the most benign situations.

The Arrogant

Arrogance is false confidence, and it always masks major insecurities. Arrogant people tend to be disagreeable low performers, and have more cognitive problems than the average person. Arrogant people see everything you do as a personal challenge.

The Group-Thinker

Group-Thinkers choose the path of least resistance and are famous for propagating a "this is how we've always done it" mentality. If you find yourself getting brainwashed with what everyone else believes, be careful. The status quo never leads to greatness.

The Short-Changed

The short-changed are quick to blame their lack of accomplishment on a lack of opportunity. While a lucky break may give a little wind to a successful person's sail, they got where they are through demanding work. What the short-changed don't realize is that their attitude is what is short-changing them—not their circumstances.

The Temperamental

Temperamental people perform poorly because their emotions cloud their judgement, and their lack of self-control destroys their relationships. They will lash out at you and project their feelings onto you, all the while thinking you are the one causing their malaise. Be wary of temperamental people when push comes to shove. They will use you as their emotional toilet.

The Victim

Victims are tough to identify because you initially empathize with their problems. But as time passes, you begin to realize that their "time of need" is all of the time. Victims actively push away any personal responsibility by making every speed bump they encounter into an uncrossable mountain. They don't see tough times as opportunities to learn. Instead, they use them as an out.

The Gullible

You can't help but feel sorry for the gullible types. They are the ones who find themselves babysitting the boss's kids the morning after pulling a late night of work! For whatever reason, gullible people (often newbies) go with the flow until the gentle river becomes a tumultuous ocean. It is okay to negotiate your salary, to say no, and to question tradition.

The Apologizer

For every person out there who owes an apology, there is another who apologizes too often. They fear failure and believe that apologizing will act as a safety net. Instead, unnecessary apologies cheapen their ideas and make them less likely to stick. Stating an idea or opinion as a question is just as bad as apologizing.

The good news is that these behaviors can be eradicated through emotional intelligence. All it takes is a little self-awareness and an ardent desire to change. John Wooten said, "Failure isn't fatal, but failure to change might be." Alvin Toffler said, "The illiterate of the twenty-first century will not be those cannot read and write, but those who cannot learn, unlearn, and relearn." As a passion-driven leader, you have to be the change that you want to see in others. Goethe said, "Treat people as if they were what they ought to be and you help them become what they are capable of becoming."

The way we express emotions are core elements of our leadership style and presence. Our emotions are influenced by our personality, as well as the skills we possess. Some researchers suggest that emotional intelligence is the strongest predictor of job performance, and that 90% of top performers have high emotional intelligence. This includes all fields, at all levels, in every region of the world (Bradberry and Greaves).[58] The good news is that emotional intelligence is a set of learned abilities. In other words, we can learn these skills and become more emotionally intelligent.

According to Goleman, Boyatzis, and McKee, there are four components of EI: self-awareness, self- management, social awareness, and social management.[59]

Self-awareness is the ability to recognize your own feelings and name them. It also allows you to recognize the impact of your emotions, to know your strengths and limits, and to have self-confidence.

Self-management is the ability to consciously respond to emotions. Self-management includes emotional self-control, transparency, adaptability, initiative, and readiness to act and seize opportunities. It allows you to anticipate consequences and respond to an emotion in a way that feels aligned to your values' social context. It doesn't mean that you suppress feelings. It means that you make conscious choices. When emotional management is underdeveloped, we can get consumed by our feelings.

Social awareness is the ability to recognize and understand the feelings of others. Social awareness includes empathy, organization awareness, and service.

Social management, or relationship management, is the ability to manage conflict, form healthy relationships, collaborate, offer feedback and guidance, and motivate and inspire others. Even though all the components of EI build on each other, it is important to manage your emotions effectively. If you are not aware of your emotions, navigating other relationships becomes difficult. Emotional intelligence is the foundation of trusting relationships, interpersonal communication, flexibility, time management, empathy, decision making, collaboration, presentation, skills, assertiveness, regulating stress, managing anger, and resilience.

Passion-driven leaders realize that emotional intelligence isn't about suppressing, controlling, or eliminating emotions. It's about recognizing your range of emotions and making thoughtful choices about how to respond. They constantly model the behaviors they want to see in their team. They also engage in daily reflection because they realize it is a primary vehicle for cultivating emotional intelligence, as well as mental and spiritual growth. You can't grow your organization or your leadership team if you won't grow yourself. Trust is the feeling of confidence we have in another's character and competence (Covey).[60] And to cultivate trust, we need to know ourselves as leaders. Megan Tschannen-Moran defines trust as "a state in which individuals and groups, are willing to make themselves vulnerable to others and take risk with confidence that others will respond to their actions in positive ways, that is, with benevolence, predictability, competence, honesty, and openness." Aguilar).[61]

As you reflect on this chapter, ask yourself the following questions:

- *Where am I regarding my emotional intelligence?*
- *How do I handle my temperament? Do I have the temperament and emotional intelligence to grow other leaders?*
- *Am I leading in such a way that others truly trust me?*
- *What changes do I need to make to grow?*
- *What changes do I need to make to position myself to grow others?*

CHAPTER

THE BRANDING PROCESS: YOU ARE THE BRAND

Before you are a leader success is all about growing yourself but when you become a leader, success is all about growing others.
—Jack Welch

If you are the principal of a Title I school, you must realize you are the brand for that school. In other words, you are the image/face of the school. You must also craft the message, and that message must be your vision for the school's success.

We are exposed to messages and brands every day. In fact, every time you hear a commercial you are exposed to message and brand. I grew up eating Frosted Flakes® because Tony the Tiger® (brand) said, "They're grrrreat!" (message). Although I am a vegetarian with vegan tendencies, I sometimes crave a three-piece mixed crispy and original chicken with cole slaw, mashed potatoes, and a biscuit because Colonel Sanders said, "It's finger lickin' good" (message). I often get a Whopper® without meat at Burger King® because the King (brand) told me I could "have it my way at Burger King®'" (message).

Fortune 500 companies figured out a long time ago that the best way to sell a product is to create a marketable brand combined with a catchy phrase, because image and perception is everything when it comes to sales. Remember, perception is a form of data. As the principal, you get a chance to alter the perception of your school. In my opinion, there are two reasons why this is important. In the black community, there are basically two institutions that we have counted on for guidance: the church (pastor) and the school (principal). Unfortunately, due to the ever-changing landscape of accountability, most schools in our communities struggle with meeting the assessment measures set before them and are labeled as "failing schools." Bogin and Nhuyen-Hoang found that when Title I schools failed to meet AYP for two years (and were therefore deemed failing), home values decreased. The stigma associated with living in these high-need areas also increased.[62]

This problem is compounded by the fact that the media spreads messages of gross inequity and inequality by not informing viewers of the whole story—or as Paul Harvey would say, the moral of the story.

This taints the public's perception of our schools, which is why principals must become the brand and constantly communicate a simple but powerful message. If you are at a school for five years or more, your message will likely change. Like Coca-Cola, you must find a way to transform your message and keep it relevant to your school's growth. When I was little boy in the 60s and 70s, we had Coke and Diet Coke. Now there is classic Coke, Vanilla Coke, Cherry Coke, Coke Zero Sugar, Coca-Cola Life, Caffeine-Free Diet Coke, and Coke Zero Sugar Cherry. The net worth of Coca-Cola is $171.81 billion, in part because they have mastered the art of brand and message.

BE THE BRAND

Being the brand means you must be the change you want to see in others. After all, as is the principal, so is the school. Therefore, you must dress accordingly. I'm not suggesting that you need to dress like you are on the cover of *Vogue*, but when folks come to campus, your clothes should distinguish you from the custodian, gym teacher, or secretary. John C. Maxwell once said, "A leader knows the way, goes the way, and shows the way."[63] In other words, if your leadership style is not transformational, then you need to become transformational. Transformational leaders have the ability to positively change those with whom they work. As I mentioned in the last chapter, you can't grow your company, organization, business, or those on your leadership team if you won't grow yourself. Futurist Alvin Toffler said, "The illiterate of the twenty- first century will not be those who cannot read or write, but those who cannot learn, unlearn, and relearn" (Finzel).[64] You are the brand, so if you want your staff to come early and stay late, then you have to do the same. Not only that, but you have to communicate why in a positive way. If you want teachers to exemplify professionalism even when parents are being rude to them, then you are going to have to model that for them. Being the brand is nothing more than the gradual release model for adults:

- I do.
- We do.
- You do.

The key to transforming adults is the same as it is for children. Great teachers know that children don't care how much you know until they know how much you care. It works the same with adults—they call it trust. In fact, research by Hoy suggests that faculty trust in student and parents is related to increased student achievement, despite socio-economic status. They define trust as "a state in which individuals and groups are willing to make themselves vulnerable to others and take risks with confidence that others will respond to their actions in positive ways, that is, with benevolence, predictability, competence, honesty, and openness."[65] This is the essence of academic optimism, which we will explore in Chapter 4. As the brand, you must model that trust for them.

In his book *You are the Brand,* Steve Adubato suggests the following:

- Your customers must trust you and your product/service. They must feel that you know and understand them and their needs. If they trust in these things, they will be loyal customers.

- The brand of the company must be strong enough to give value to the individuals within it. Remember that no one is expendable—not even the biggest and most popular star or brand.

- Taking the time to remain accessible and friendly matters. Do what you do with a smile and upbeat attitude. Your brand is greatly influenced by your demeanor, not just your technical skills.[66]

You can do this by doing simple things, such as saying good morning and thank you, even when you don't feel like it. You can stand in the front of the school and greet parents and students in the morning, and say good-bye after school. You can also publicly recognize stakeholders when they do something well, and privately tell them when they haven't.

You should only have faculty meetings for necessary items and send other important items in an email. This conveys the message that you value their time and yours. Give teachers honest and consistent feedback. Be honest with district personnel when they want you to implement a program or process that you know is not the best fit for your school. Remember, every person is perfectly aligned for the trust that they give.

THE MESSAGE

The message needs to reflect your vision. It needs to be a simple phrase, and not a paragraph. You need to communicate it daily to all stakeholders. It needs to be part of the morning and evening announcements on the intercom. If you are the principal at the same school for three or more years, your message will—and should—change. As the culture and climate change, so should your message, which conveys your vision. Gillian Williams, Founder and former President of School Turnaround, suggests that your message should.[67]:

- Connect to targets. Strong messages are aligned to your goals. For example, your target could be, "success: twenty-four by fifteen," meaning twenty-four classrooms were going to average 15% gains.

- Use positive language. This means you don't use phrases like, "Failure is not an option."

From	To
Accountability	Performance
Compliance	Responsibility
Monitoring	Helping
Evaluating	Verifying

- Be individualized and idiosyncratic. Your message should not be generic or even readily understandable to the outside world, and you can`t buy it in a store or a catalogue.
- Be timely. It must be relevant to what is happening in your school now.
- Geared to intervene. How can the message be used in a way to intervene in small and big ways? Think about what is blocking high achievement at your school.
- Personal to leadership. It has to fit the school leader's personality and style. Remember the message is the rallying cry for the school. In order for it to be effective, it has to ring true to the school leader.

Williams also states that there are three kinds of people in most organizations:

- **Early adapters.** This is the small group (10-15%) of your school staff that will be the first to change what they think and do.

- **Mainstream.** These are the people (70-80%) who will not be first, but they are not far behind. There are two groups within the mainstream. The first group has to see others accept change. The second group has a reason why they won't adapt, so you have to figure out what it is and address it.

- **Laggards.** These people (5-10%) are very resistant to change. They tend to repeat concerns and criticisms even when asking questions. You may or may not get them hooked on change later. In any case, avoid rising to the bait they may toss at you. They are the last people to spend your time persuading.

Remember, you must be the change that you want to see in others at your school. According to Kouzes and Posner, "leadership is not about personality; it's about behavior."[68] According to Hans Finzel, "Leadership is influence. A leader takes people where they would never go on their own."[69] After all, as is the principal so is the school!

CHAPTER

BEYOND TURNAROUND

*The worst mistake a leader can make is to
surround themselves with people who have
small minds thinking miniscule thoughts
on a microscopic level.*
—T.D. Burton

I devoted an entire chapter to this subject because it is such an important skill set for principals to develop. If the principal is going to survive past the turnaround process, which takes about two years, they must develop a skill set that will enable them to build capacity and recruit and retain teachers. In other words, when the brand and message work synergistically, it creates a climate of academic optimism, collective efficacy, and trust that will result in increased student achievement and a capacity for teachers to grow and recruit other likeminded teachers.

Efficacy is the belief faculty can make a positive contribution to student learning—teachers believe in themselves. Collective efficacy is the belief that teachers (as a collective) have a sense that they can organize and execute decisions and influence the activities that have positive effects on students. As mentioned in the previous chapter, trust is "a state in which individuals and groups are willing to make themselves vulnerable to others and take risks with confidence that others will respond to their actions in positive ways, that is, with benevolence, predictability, competence, honesty, and openness" (Hoy).[70] Academic emphasis is the academic enactment of these beliefs — teachers act to improve academic success of students.

Academic optimism is the uniting of these three concepts into an integrated whole. It is the collective belief that:

- The faculty can make a difference (cognitive).
- Students can learn (affective and emotional).
- Academic performance can be achieved (behavioral).

In fact, Hoy suggest that academic optimism is a stronger indicator of high student achievement than socio-economic status.[71] Gillian Williams, Founder and former President of School Turnaround, once stated in a training meeting, "Turnaround is not a place to hang out at!" Likewise, I am suggesting that leading beyond turnaround takes a different skill set that involves building capacity by engaging in academic optimism, as well as recruiting and retaining teachers. Well, if academic optimism is the *what*, how does it happen? Remember that every person is perfectly aligned for the trust that they give.

Bridges of trust are built by principals who set high expectations for themselves as well as their teachers, because they realize that no one rises to low expectations. They reinforce this by constantly communicating their expectations and demonstrating their effort to grow.

Trust is built by simple things, like smiling and saying good morning—even when you don't feel like it. People trust consistency. You can't lead with your emotions, good or bad (as discussed in Chapter 2).

Trust is built by giving teachers constructive feedback as they set challenging goals for themselves, and providing relevant professional development opportunities.

RECRUIT AND RETAIN

Every school system has a job fair at least once a year. If that is only time you recruit teachers, then you will be woefully behind the eight ball regarding staffing. Recruitment is a year-round process that occurs daily. My principal friends would often not let me talk to their teachers because they knew my motto: "All is fair in love, war, and stealing good teachers." I would actively recruit those whom I perceived to be their best teachers. I became an adjunct professor in the department of education at two local universities, so I could create my own pipeline of new teachers. The truth is, once you have established a culture of academic optimism, you won`t have to recruit. Your teachers will do it for you.

"A great principal, just like any other manager, is critical to retention because, as noted earlier, most people don't leave organizations, they leave supervisors" (Gordon and Crabtree).[72] Therefore, it is important that principals focus on recruiting and retaining teachers.

Teachers have a more significant influence on student achievement than any other aspect of the school, and they vary widely in their impact (Kane, Rockoff, and Staiger 2006; Nye, Konstantopolous, and Hedges).[73]

Poor and minority students are more likely to be assigned teachers who have less experience, or who are teaching without full certification. This negatively influences their ability to produce high levels of student learning (Clotfelter, Ladd, and Vigdor).[74]

According to a 2009 report from the U.S. Department of Education's Office of Planning, Evaluation, and Policy Development, 57% of high-poverty schools made adequate yearly progress (AYP) in 2004, compared to 84% of low-poverty schools. Although teachers were required to be designated as highly qualified under The No Child Left Behind Act of 2001 (NCLB), "teachers in high-poverty schools had less experience and were less likely to have a degree in the subject that they teach" (p. 3).[75]

Good teaching is not an accident. While some teachers are more naturally gifted than others, all effective teaching is the result of study, reflection, practice, and hard work (Marzano, Waters, and McNulty).[76] However, teachers need to feel valued, a place where they can grow as leaders, and a learning environment where they feel safe.

A growing body of evidence suggests that schools can make a great difference in terms of student achievement, and a substantial portion of that difference is attributed to teachers. Specifically, teacher effectiveness is a strong determinant of differences in student learning, far outweighing the effects of differences in class size and class heterogeneity. Students who are assigned to one ineffective teacher after another have significant losses n achievement and learning compared to those who are assigned to a sequence of several highly effective teachers. (Saunders and Rivers 1996).[77] Thus, the impact of teacher effectiveness or ineffectiveness seems to be additive or cumulative.

THE ROLE OF THE PRINCIPAL IN TEACHER RETENTION

The role and responsibility of the principal is to understand the group dynamics of teachers and help them develop a sense of innovation. Effective communication, which Stephen Covey argues is "the most important skill in life,"[78] is key to the successful implementation of any new program.

Many studies on leadership list communication as the top skill of successful leaders (Gardner and Laskin; Kouzes and Posner; McEwan; Maxwell; Sava 1997; Tichy).[79] School principals are who are highly successful communicate practically all of their working hours (Elmore).[80] Thus, effective communication consists of a wide variety of behaviors other than talking, such as listening, writing, and reading. This also includes body language. In this respect, effective communication is an art form, a dance of connection that, according to Learner, coordinates all of these different skills into one complex act.[81]

Sergiovanni argued, "The heart of leadership has to do with what a person believes, values, dreams about and is committed to the person's personal vision."[82] Effective principals emphasize emotional and interpersonal relationships instead of bureaucracy (Elmore).[83] Cotton argues that strong school leaders will recognize the achievements of students and staff and use them to augment a positive and supportive atmosphere.[84] Marzano, Waters and McNulty call this "affirmation and contingent awards."[85] Such a culture places a high value on school ritual, ceremony and tradition. Cotton also couples the ability to build a positive culture with vision, arguing that in order to create an effective environment, a learner must have a well-developed vision that includes more than student academic achievement.[86] Marzano, Waters, and McNulty take this a step further, explaining that a vision and a culture cannot exist solely in principle.[87] The school leader must show members of the school, through words and actions, what traits or behaviors are valued (*TAP Handbook*).[88]

Fullan stated that true leaders do not overwhelm others by being Superman or creating dependency.[89] They use the power of the positive culture they have developed and involve as many people as possible to reach their goals. They respect the people who resist change, and then seek to understand and address their resistance (McEwan).[90] In short, leaders have to be highly flexible masters of change, and use their vision to help motivate others. They instill trust with thoughtful and consistent arguments and actions, thus enabling others to act (Kouzes and Posner).[91] They bolster confidence in their vision by celebrating incremental steps along the way. The true change master is able to manage change so that it is organized, resulting in a more positive, powerful, and sustainable environment (*TAP Handbook*).[92]

Kenneth Leithwood and Carolyn Riehl described effective leaders as those who know what they were not, and then construct a focused and systematic plan to achieve the goals they set for themselves.[93] Thus, while administrators do need to manage and direct staff, their primary responsibility should be understanding and becoming involved the subject matter and pedagogy of the school (Stein and D'Amico).[94] When this is done, the faculty will be inspired to accomplish things that might otherwise be beyond their grasp (Marzano, Waters, and McNulty; *TAP Handbook*).[95] Teachers tend to demonstrate high self-efficacy when communication with the principal is regular, open, and honest (Gimbal).[96]

Zimmerman found that high levels of communication between administration and staff correlated positively with high teacher self-efficacy.[97] Studies conducted by Blasé and Blasé and Gimel indicated that teacher input into decision-making is important for building principal–teacher trust.[98] These same authors propose that an open and honest climate is conducive for teacher growth. However, data suggest that such a climate is valued among principals, but less valued among teachers. Youngs and King, Gimel, and Zimmerman suggested that to enhance teacher growth, principals should solicit input from their teachers when making decisions.[99] They should also maintain open communication with all teachers, new and veteran, and engage them in conversations about instructional practice.

Primarily, principals should observe and offer effective, timely feedback to teachers about their instructional practices. Secondly, the principal's role in providing a mentor, especially to new and beginning teachers, is important. Data from this exploratory study suggest that the mentors are important to teacher development. Lastly, principals should look for effective teachers to serve as mentors and provide training. The quality of the teacher mentor, the mentor–protégé relationship, and training all contribute to the professional growth of the teacher (Jueves).[100]

They should acknowledge that collaboration is worthwhile, and it can work. It will not work, however, if a school's leader does not put a great deal of work, planning, and trust into it (Daane et al.).[101] The collaboration process should begin by reviewing data and gathering input from teachers, curriculum staff, and consultants.

To facilitate the process of effective job-embedded professional development, Rogers refers to the principal's role and responsibility as that of change agent or opinion leader.[102] He states that attitudes are developed through communication about the innovation of peers and opinion leaders. Ongoing learning is an essential component of continuous improvement for teachers (Barber and Mourshed).[103]

Unfortunately, too many professional learning activities are disconnected from teachers' actual practice and school improvement goals (Cohen and Hill; Kennedy 1998).[104] They are not designed for the needs of adult learners (Croft, Coggshall, Dolan, and Powers).[105]

What attracts teachers to professional development, therefore, is their belief that it will expand their knowledge and skills, contribute to their growth, and enhance their effectiveness with students. However, teachers also tend to be quite pragmatic. What they hope to gain through professional development are specific, concrete, and practical ideas that directly relate to the day-to-day operation of their classrooms (Fullan and Miles).[106] Development programs that fail to address these needs are unlikely to succeed (Guskey).[107]

The content of the professional development is most useful when it focuses on "concrete tasks of teaching, assessments, observation and reflection" (Darling-Hammond and McLahghlin), rather than abstract discussion of teaching.[108] Studies show professional development is most effective when it focuses on enhancing teachers' knowledge of how to engage in specific pedagogical skills and how to teach specific kinds of content to learners. Equally important is a focus on student learning, including an analysis of concepts and skills that students are expected to demonstrate (Carpenter et al. 1989).[109]

High-quality professional development is a central component in nearly every modern proposal for improving education. Policy makers increasingly recognize that schools can be no better than their teachers and administrators. While these proposed professional development programs vary widely in content and format, most share a common purpose: to "alter the professional practices, beliefs and understanding of school personnel toward an articulated end" (Griffin).[110]

I found that when I was dedicated to teachers' growth, I didn't have to recruit. They did it for me, because they had established a standard of excellence and wanted to work with like-minded teachers. Hence, the culture and climate changed to one of perpetual excellence. Did we have problems? Of course. But we collectively chose to survive and thrive, which we often referred to as "surthrival." In my opinion, there are basically two ways to improve student achievement. One is selective student enrollment, catering to only the best and brightest. The other is to help your teachers grow. Title I schools can't select students, but effective leaders have an obligation to be the change we want to see in teachers. When we see them, we should see greatness.

PERSISTENCE THROUGH PROBLEMS

It has been said that God takes care of babies and fools. I`m convince that God, in His infinite wisdom, knew that I would need more than one mother. He sent me two moms because I usually fall into the "fool" category. I was blessed to be raised by Claudette Calhoun Burton, a single mom and first grade teacher who instilled in us confidence that we could do and be anything that we wanted to be. She held us to a standard of excellence that still permeates the very fiber of our being. When she passed away, I had a void in my life as deep as the Grand Canyon. Little did I know that God had already prepared a surrogate mom for me through Marie Clark.

Mrs. Clark was the director of school performance while I was an elementary school principal. In other words, she was my boss. The problem was I assumed that my skill set as an assistant principal was adequate to be an effective principal, so I was rather arrogant and cocky. And like my biological mom, who spanked me physically, Mrs. Clark spanked me with "pen, paper, love, and consistency." Many of her lessons made me the leader I am today. One of the many things she told me was, "Mr. Burton, the problems in your building aren't going away, so you have to deal with them head on." As an assistant principal, I was used to dealing with student issues, irate parents, and support services issues. I was very comfortable with confrontation, but I had a lot of growing to do on the instructional side of the school house. She not only told me how to handle these problems, but in true educational form, she modeled it. So, let me tell you that the problems in your buildings aren't going away. Become comfortable with confrontation, and develop an eye for quality instruction.

To consistently and effectively deal with the problems in my building, I had to find my voice. To find my style of leadership, I had to reflect on my strengths and weaknesses. Stacy Brown, the CEO and founder of Chicken Salad Chic, once said, "Don't be afraid of weaknesses. If there are things you aren't good at, surround yourself with people who have a passion for what your weaknesses are." They key word in the last sentence is "passion." The leadership styles that are most commonly referred to are transformational, transactional, servant, invitational, and passive/avoidant (also known as laissez-faire).

Transformational leadership is "a process of influencing in which leaders change their associates' awareness of what is important and move them to see themselves and the opportunities and challenges of their environment in a new way" (Bass and Avolio, 1994).[111]

Transformational leaders have a vision for the future of the school organization, effectively communicate that vision to followers, and inspire followers to deeply commit and work interdependently towards its attainment (Cooper et al.).[112] Past research showed "teachers strongly preferred behaviors that aligned with the aspects of transformational leadership" (Hauserman and Stick).[113] The importance of this finding is that principals' actions influence teachers' attitudes "High functioning schools were found to have transformational principals who shaped the school vision and learning processes within the organization, thus creating a positive learning culture" (Hauserman and Stick 2013).[114] Highly transformational principals developed the leadership skills of all staff, encouraged reflection, assisted with problems, emphasized teamwork and collegiality, and pushed staff to think outside the box (Hauserman and Stick).[115]

According to research, "transformational leadership engages in the creating of a shared interest that unites leaders and followers" (Bass 1999).[116] There are four components of transformational leadership: idealized influence or charisma, inspirational motivation, intellectual stimulation, and individualized consideration Idealized influence or charisma includes two components. First, "followers attribute the leader with certain qualities that followers wish to emulate." Second, "leaders impress followers through their behaviors." Transformational leaders are able to approach common problems in innovative ways. This means their followers are also creative risk-takers, which is intellectual stimulation. Individual consideration is a leader taking an authentic interest in the followers' personal or professional goals (Cooper 2012).[117]

Transactional leadership focuses on results, conforms to the existing structure of an organization, and measures success according to the organization's system of rewards and penalties. Transactional leaders "define expectations and promote performance to achieve these levels."[118] Transactional leaders have formal authority and positions of responsibility. This type of leader is responsible for maintaining routine by managing individual performance and facilitating group performance. Transactional leadership is most often compared to transformational leadership. Transactional leadership depends on self-motivated people who work well in a structured, directed environment. By contrast, transformational leadership seeks to motivate and inspire workers, choosing to influence rather than direct. (St Thomas University).[119]

The servant leadership theory is rooted in ethical and caring behavior. Employees' well-being is given high priority (van Dierendonck 2011).[120] Greenleaf stated, "Servant-leaders differ from other persons of goodwill because they act on what they believe. Consequently, they 'know experimentally' and there is a sustaining spirit when they venture and risk. To the worldly, servant-leaders may seem naïve; and they may not adapt readily to prevailing institutional structures."[121] In a qualitative study of servant leaders, researchers identified several themes: being interpersonal, character, problem-solving, work habits, inspired leadership, and self-assurance (Hamilton and Knoche).[122]

A newer theory with a positive and encouraging structure is invitational leadership. William Purkey and Betty Siegel designed this theory in 2002.[123] The invitational leadership theory is based on four components: optimism, respect, trust, and intentionality. Hope is an important element to success in educational organizations, and was added to the components in a more recent study (Purkey and Novak).[124] Respect is a basic human need that affirms people's value. Trust is crucial in the success of an organization. Invitational leaders are intentional, and have purpose in their work and relationships. Processes that require cooperation and positivity builds effective teams. The five P's to invite other professionals in the invitational leadership theory are "people, places, policies, programs, and processes" (Purkey & Siegel 2002).[125]

Passive/avoidant leaders are reactive. They "avoid specifying agreements, clarifying expectations, and providing goals and standards to be achieved by followers."[126]

Bass and Avolio (1994) defined passive/avoidant leadership as having "a negative effect on desired outcomes—opposite to what is intended by the leader-manager. In this regard it is similar to laissez-faire styles—or 'no leadership.'"[127] The characteristics most associated with passive/avoidant leadership are passive exception and laissez-faire attitudes.

While developing my style of leadership, I had to learn a few things. I had to learn that there is a difference good principals and great principals. Great principals know how to lead, follow, and get out of the way. Transformation is a process that happens in degrees of time. You may not be a transformational leader at the onset of your principalship, but there need to be signs that construction is underway. Transformation starts in your mind first. It is intrinsic before it ever becomes extrinsic. My leadership team changed three times while I was a principal, and as I transformed, my role changed. The way I led throughout my last few years as a principal was completely different than the first three years.

I had to learn that leadership is a process. "It's difficult for leaders to be effective if they do not take the time to examine their sense of purpose and the ways it has been defined, influenced, informed and refined by their experiences" (Green).[128] A leader working on their own dispositions is a learning process, heavily based on the learner's reflection and self-assessment (Green).[129]

I had to learn that when principals actively lead and change school conditions related to governance structure, school culture, retention policies, curriculum adherence, and working conditions, variations in student achievement may occur (Leithwood, Seashore, Anderson, and Wahlstrom 2004).[130]

I had to learn that the role of the public school principal is to create a learning environment that provides high-quality educational programming and instruction for students, in spite of strong correlations between socioeconomic status and academic performance.

Ylimaki found evidence that suggests "principals who made a difference in high-poverty schools exhibited similar traits of persistence, empathy, passion, and flexible, creative thinking."[131] I had to learn to become a transformational, passion-driven leader, because students' lives were at stake.

ADAPTIVE VERSUS TECHNICAL

Trust is built when principals are resilient and persistent, such as when they address custodial needs or repair technology. This indicates that you are an efficient problem solver.

The reason why problems aren't addressed adequately at some schools is because some leaders have a chain of interaction, rather than a chain of command. These look alike in that they both define roles and responsibilities of administrators, as well as who staff should report to. The difference is that in a chain of interaction, staff talk to administrators even if they are not the ones who are responsible for getting that specific issue solved. In a chain of command, staff only reports issues to the administrators who are responsible for handling those issues in their respective wheel wells. The chain of interaction is not the best alignment of resources, nor is it very productive. The chain of command reinforces order and resource alignment, and is an effective use of the Structural frame.

Keep in mind that all problems are adaptive, technical, or a mixture of the two. However, in dealing with any problem, you must become comfortable with confrontation. If confrontation makes you uncomfortable, then you won't do well as a principal.

Kind of Challenge	Problem Definition	Solution	Focus of Work
Technical	Clear	Clear	Authority
Technical and Adaptive	Clear	Requires Learning	Authority and Stakeholders
Adaptive	Requires Learning	Requires Learning	Stakeholders

Technical

- complex
- critically important
- known solutions
- implemented with current know-how
- resolved through authoritative expertise
- current structures, procedures, and ways of doing things

Adaptive

- changes in people's priorities, beliefs, habits, and loyalties
- goes beyond authoritative expertise to mobilize discovery
- sheds certain entrenched ways
- may threaten success
- Tolerates losses
- Generates new capacity to thrive

Adaptive leadership means looking forward and backward at the same time. It means putting to rest traumas of the past, embracing new ways of doing business, and tackling pressing issues by developing adaptive solutions. Realize that organizational problems are often structural, not personal, even when they take on personal tones. That's why diagnosing the problem is the most important part of adaptive leadership. You must remain steady to diagnose the problem. You must get on the balcony and get a distanced perspective of what is really happening throughout an organization or group. Adaptive leadership is specifically about change that enables the ability to thrive. Successful changes build on the past rather than jettison it. Adaptation relies on diversity. New adaptations significantly displace, reregulate, and rearrange some old DNA.

Any social system is the way it is because the people in that system want it that way—or at least, the people with most leverage want it that way. That is why mastering the two are important.

CHAPTER

DATA-DRIVEN OR DATA-INFORMED?

*Every organization is perfectly aligned for
the results that it gets.*
—Stephen Kukic

This chapter is probably the shortest chapter in the book, not because it isn't important, but because there have been volumes written on this subject—most of which I tend to disagree with from a functional standpoint. My only challenge to you in this chapter is to think and rethink how you use data. The question is, are you data-driven or data-informed?

All organizations utilize data. The key, however, is not to allow yourself to become data rich and information poor. Remember, data is only as good as the questions that you ask. Does it answer the questions about your organization, and is the data relevant? Is the data aligned? Are you comparing apples to apples, or apples to oranges? As Stephen Kukic said, "Every organization is perfectly aligned for the results that it gets." All these phrases sound too familiar when talking about data. So, are you data-driven or data-informed? Let me share with you a perspective that may cause you to rethink your usage of data.

For instance, if you are sick and go to the doctor, the first thing they may ask is, "How are you feeling?" In other words, what are your symptoms? You may have a fever, and your other symptoms may include headaches, chest congestion, watery eyes, and post-nasal drip. You may even go on to tell the doctor that you think you have the flu and may need to miss a few days of school. We will call that *perception data* or *qualitative evidence* because you made the diagnosis based on your perception. In turn, your doctor should run some tests. Then, you will be sent to the lab and may have blood work or a chest x-ray done. Of course, this is after the doctor has already taken your blood pressure, checked your eyes and ears, and listened to your heart. These tests are done so the doctor can obtain what we will call *academic data* or *quantifiable evidence*. Before you receive your test results, the doctor may look at your chart and discuss past office visits, or look at your family history to see if certain diseases run in your family. He may even suggest that certain diseases are more prevalent in different races of people. We will call this *background and demographic data* which is also *quantitative evidence.*

The bottom line is that your doctor will use four kinds of data before he makes a diagnosis, or an informed decision: perception, academic, background, and demographic. Doctors are bound to make informed decisions. According to the Hippocratic oath, their priority is to "do no harm." This means that he is held liable or responsible for the treatment that he will prescribe to you based on the data. In other words, doctors use data to make informed decisions. I don`t know about you, but when I am sick, I want my doctor to use data and make informed decisions so I can get better.

In the wonderful world of education, the buzz phrase now seems to be "data-driven." There are book, white papers, dissertations, and theses written on how to make data-driven decisions. Like the good doctor, we use academic data such as report cards, DIBELS, STAR360, NAEP, Aimsweb, benchmark assessments, and standardized tests. We will use cumulative records of students to obtain background and demographic data. And God forbid, if a school becomes labeled as a "failing school," districts use parent, teacher, and student surveys so they can get their perception of the problem. Then, they attend meetings and allow the data to drive their decisions regarding school business. We have so much data that we are data rich and information poor. The most damning part about being data-driven is that it absolves all involved parties of any responsibility. We proudly say, "according to the data" or "the data made me do it." Winston Churchill said, "The price of greatness is responsibility." Why not strive to be great instead of good?

I know as educators, we don't take the Hippocratic oath, but it makes sense for us to make informed decisions instead of being data-driven. As educators we deal with the most valuable resource that our country has, and it behoove us to first "do no harm," especially to those who are under-resourced academically and socially. Aristotle said, "The educated differ from the uneducated as much as the living from the dead." Being data-driven gives us latitude to undereducated decisions regarding students who are already under-resourced academically. I suggest that we all strive to make decisions that are data-informed.

EVIDENCE-BASED LEADING

It is important to note that activity and progress are two different things, so "cut the fluff." This is another term that Mrs. Clark used quite frequently. Some organizations now refer to it as "resource alignment." She was way ahead of her time. Evidence-based leading (EBL) is a term that I use when discussing resource alignment, or cutting the fluff. According to the Oxford Review article "The Essential Guide to Evidence- Based Leadership," EBL refers to the process and practice of using "best evidence" and "hard facts" about the current situation.[132] It also involves decision-making skills. This means being able to separate facts from half-truths, pet theories, unfounded beliefs, and the just plain wrong that often masquerades as good leadership advice and practice. The first question to ask as you make decisions is, "Where is the evidence?" I know this practice is used commonly in the healthcare field, but what more important field to use it than education, where lives are also at stake?

When the district suggests that you implement a new program, please have the courage to demand empirical evidence, and ask if it has worked for similar student populations. In my opinion, we have an obligation to lead using empirically research-based evidence. I consider anything less to be educational malpractice.

CHAPTER

6

THE BALANCING ACT: THE VICISSITUDES OF LIFE (VOL)

*Passion-driven leaders make purposeful
decisions and have the ability to persevere
when things go wrong.*
— T.D. Burton

The "vicissitudes of life" are normally difficult times that we all go through: sickness, job loss, and other unwelcomed episodes. To survive the vicissitudes of life means to survive life's ups and downs—with a special emphasis on the downs. *Vicissitude* is a descendant of the Latin noun *vicis*, meaning "change" or "alternation." This chapter is relevant to me personally because it was an area that I struggled with for years. I was the poster boy for workaholics, and let me tell you, it was a lonely life. I was successful in my career, so my colleagues assumed that I was doing well personally.

Nothing could have been farther from the truth. This is why the title of this chapter is "The Balancing Act," with the key word being "balance." In fact, I could have written an entire book on the mistakes I made by not having balance. Life has taught me some very valuable lessons regarding balance, such as:

- When stressed, most leaders will develop either a vice or virtue.
- There is a difference between coping with stress and managing stress.
- No one will take care of you like you.
- You aren't any good to anyone else unless you are good to yourself first.
- People you lead will respect you more when you take care of yourself.
- Achieving balance means being completely honest with yourself regarding every aspect of your life.

Leaders lead complicated, demanding lives, so it is important to make a conscious effort to reflect on your various roles. There is a very close correlation between your emotional intelligence, your personality, and the skill set that you will you learn in this chapter. In fact, if you are well-grounded emotionally and have a firm grasp on your personality/inner self, the more balanced you will be. The three culprits that contribute to leaders being out of balance are:

- stress
- emotional bank accounts
- knowing your roles

I call them the three amigos (friends), any one of which can cause unbalance to occur. But if all three friends roll up on you at the same time, you may as well get ready to rumble, because your life will be topsy-turvy every day!

Stress is a state of disharmony or a threat to homeostasis. Stress is your body's way of responding to any kind of demand or threat. Stress is your body's way of protecting you. When you sense danger, real or imagined, your body's defense mechanism kicks in to high gear, which is commonly known as "fight-or-flight" or the "stress response." When it is working properly, it helps you stay energetic and alert. In some situations, stress can save your life (for instance, stress can give you extra strength to defend yourself or cause you to slam the brakes to avoid an accident). Causal factors for stress can be external or internal.

Some external causes could be:

- major life changes
- work or school
- relationship difficulties
- financial problems
- being too busy
- children, family or church

Some internal causes could be:

- pessimism
- inability to accept uncertainty
- rigid thinking, lack of flexibility
- negative self-talk
- unrealistic expectations/perfectionism
- all-or-nothing attitude

To some degree, stress depends on a person's perception. What causes stress to one person may not faze another— hence the need to know your personality type and emotional intelligence. Just as there are five levels of leadership, there are distinct levels of stress. They are:

- Eustress—managing stress can lead to growth and enhanced competence
- Distress—uncontrollable, prolonged or overwhelming stress that is destructive
- Acute stress—immediate response to a threat or challenge
- Chronic stress —ongoing, unrelenting stress

Research by Hans Selye suggests that the stages of stress response are:

- Alarm—when one feels threatened, fight-or-flight is activated
- Resistance — mobilization or resources to solve the

problem, causing adaptation

- Exhaustion—when adaptation fails and the level of function decreases[133]

You can function at the resistance stage during acute or chronic stress, because adaptation kicks in and adaptation causes coping. The three forms of coping are adaptive, active, and maladaptive. It is at this stage that I contend most leaders will develop a vice or virtue. In most cases, leaders will find a way to engage in adaptive coping or active coping. Adaptive coping (virtue) occurs when you find ways to resolve the stress response. Active coping (virtue) occurs when you actively seek a resolution to stress. Both adaptive and active coping often cause leaders to become virtuous. However, the other form of coping, maladaptation (vice), occurs when the strategies the leader chooses to cope with stress causes further problems.

For example, if you must go to happy hour every day, you might have a vice. If your happy hour starts before you get to work and continues throughout the day, you may have a vice. If you are smoking cigarettes all day and have the patch, you may have a vice. If you must smoke some marijuana every day after work, you may have a vice. If you were a weekend warrior regarding exercise and all of sudden you are running five miles before work, two miles at lunch, ten miles after work, and marathon the weekends, you may have a vice.

Stress compounds problems when leaders stay at the exhaustion stage, which manifests itself as chronic stress. This happens because the demands of the stressors exceed the leader's ability to adapt. As a result, functioning declines and health problems occur. These are just a few of the health problems that may occur if chronic stress goes unchecked:

Cognitive Symptoms

- Memory problems
- Inability to concentrate
- Poor judgement
- Seeing only the negative
- Anxious or racing thoughts
- Constant worrying

Emotional Symptoms

- Depression or general unhappiness
- Anxiety and agitation
- Moodiness, irritability or rage
- Feeling overwhelmed
- Loneliness and isolation

Physical Symptoms

- Aches and pains
- Diarrhea or constipation
- Nausea, dizziness

- Chest pain, rapid heart rate
- Loss of sex drive
- Frequent colds or flu

<u>**Behavioral Symptoms**</u>
- Eating more or less
- Sleeping too much or too little
- Withdrawing from others
- Procrastinating or neglecting responsibilities
- Using alcohol, cigarettes, or drugs to relax
- Nervous habits such as nail biting or pacing

Allow me to suggest an alternative, which is managing stress as opposed to coping with stress. The managing principles I propose for passion-driven leaders are the eight laws of health, effectively managing your emotional bank account, and knowing your roles in life.

Epidemiology is the study of the distribution and causes of health and disease in certain populations. Nutritional epidemiology is the study of diet and how it promotes or prevents disease. When scientists such as Dan Buettner, author of *Blue Zones*, and Gary E. Fraser, author of *Diet, Life Expectancy and Chronic Disease*, studied the lives of centenarians (people who are 100 years old or older), they made some remarkable discoveries.[134] They all followed what are known as the eight laws of health.

Eight Laws of Health

1. Fresh Air
2. Sunshine
3. Temperance
4. Rest
5. Exercise
6. Water
7. Nutrition
8. Trust in a divine power

Notice that diet is just one of the eight. It was the combination of these things that contributed to their longevity. Now, I am not suggesting these laws guarantee you will live over a hundred years, but I am suggesting that as a leader, you must maintain an excellent quality of life. Remember perception data is very powerful, and those who follow you base their perception on what they see. Would you want to follow or trust a snotty-nosed, short-tempered, absent-minded leader? Remember, "Trust is the feeling of confidence we have in another's character and competence" (Covey).[135] Balance in this area means following the laws of health and realizing that life is a journey. Some days you may not get them all right, but the key is to stay the course. The mind and body connection is a powerful thing. Now that we have solved the body dilemma, give me your mind!

In the book *The Seven Habits of Highly Effective People,*

Steve Covey suggests that our emotions are like bank accounts and that everyone has an emotional bank account (EBA).[136] Like any bank account, it has basically two functions: withdrawals and deposits. He suggests that emotionally healthy people know how to manage their emotional bank accounts. Likewise, I am suggesting passion-driven leaders know how to manage their emotional bank accounts. As a leader, you are constantly making deposits. This will leave you drained unless you surround yourself with people who will make deposits into your life. Additionally, people and situations are constantly making withdrawals from your life. If not properly balanced, this could leave you in the negative emotionally.

<u>Some examples of deposits are:</u>

- Keeping promises
- Kindness, courtesies
- Clarifying expectations
- Loyalty to the absent
- Being present
- Listening empathetically
- Apologies

<u>Some examples of withdrawals are:</u>

- Breaking promises
- Unkindness, discourtesies

- Violating expectations
- Disloyalty, duplicity
- Listening through your experiences
- Pride, conceit, and arrogance

Emotional deposits and withdrawals are inevitable, especially if you operate at the levels of production, people and passion. The key is to keep your account from going in the negative and staying overdrawn. Passion-driven leaders realize the following when it comes to managing their emotional bank accounts:

- We build strong and productive relationships by making deposits in the emotional bank.
- Deposits work only when they are sincere.
- Our constant relationships require us to make the deposits.
- Building or repairing trust takes time.
- Our own deposits and withdrawals are the only things that can control a relationship.
- In dealing with students, parents, stakeholders, stockholders, church members, and administrators, the little things make a big difference.
- Every problem is an opportunity for an EBA deposit.

The last item that we must deal with in terms of achieving balance is knowing your role. In the words of the late, great Steven Covey, all you have to do is "put first things first!"[137] Knowing your role is about perspective and priority. Everyone assumes various roles in life: father, husband, son, uncle, deacon, accountant, principal, etc. Balance is achieved when you have a firm grasp on how much time and energy to put into each role.

BITTER TO BETTER

The role of the principal is not for the faint of heart. You are the catalyst for everything that happens on your campus— including the good, the bad, and the ugly. Some days it seems as if all you are doing is putting out fires, or following unfunded or under-funded initiatives with seemingly little or no support. Given, this context, it is easy to become bitter.

When the first unplanned conference you have in the morning is with an irate parent, it is easy to become bitter.

When you finally make growth on your SPS and they pull the funding, it is easy to become bitter.

When you work weekends to answer a never-ending stream of emails, only to get an email on Monday that says they can't find your response, it is easy to become bitter.

I could go on and on about reasons to become bitter; however, let me challenge you to trust the process. I know it sounds cliché, but I am a living witness that it is true. The reason why some people can't trust the process is because they don't know their purpose and believe leading is just a job. When you know your purpose, and when leading is your passion, everyday problems become bumps in the road. On the other hand, if you were appointed as the principal of a Title I school and believe it is just a job, then you will invariably become bitter. If you haven't yet, you should set five-year and ten-year professional and personal goals. When you have a clearer vision of your long-term goals, it puts the vicissitudes of life in perspective.

I will end this section by telling about you my own experience—and yes, it is going to be a little preachy. Throughout my career as an administrator, I applied for several positions that I thought would be a good fit, but I didn't get them. My last experience could have easily been the most bitter, but it was the most rewarding. It wasn't bitter because I knew my purpose. I was passionate about my role as a leader, but more importantly, I prayed and asked God to open closed doors.

I had just finished my doctorate and applied for a position I felt was a good fit. I had successfully implemented the actual process at my school for which the district was advertising. In fact, I had been recognized nationally for my work, and my dissertation was on that program. Needless to say, I felt confident throughout the interview process. To make a long story short, I wasn't the recommendation for the position. I could've easily become bitter, and with just cause, but I wasn't because I trusted the process. More specifically, I trusted God by allowing Him to open and close doors in my life. I trusted Him even when I couldn't trace Him.

A few weeks later, I interviewed for my dream job and accepted the position. By trusting the process, God closed a door I thought should have been opened, and opened a door that I didn't even know existed. Choosing to become better instead of bitter is easy when you know your purpose, follow your passion, and allow God to open and close doors.

SUCCESS WITHOUT SUCCESSORS

Hans Finzel suggests that leaders plan their departure the day they start.[138] We love to think we are unique and irreplaceable as leaders. But the fact is, we will have to move on some day and leave our legacy to someone else. The last great task of any leader is to work toward a replacement who will pick up where they left off. This task should not be left until the last year of one's tenure, but should be an ongoing process of mentorship with each crop of new leaders.

Of all the leadership transition mistakes, Finzel quotes Lyle Schaller when stating the two that occur most frequently:

- Leaders tend to stay too long in a position rather than not long enough.
- Leaders who stay too long do much more damage than those who don't stay long enough (Finzel).[139]

Research by Finzel also indicates that finishing well is an important measure of success in leadership, and mentoring is a nonnegotiable function in successful leadership.[140] There are a myriad of reasons why leaders don't leave, but the truth is no one is indispensable, and we all have to let go.

What makes a good mentor? According to Stanley and Clinton, people who influence subsequent generations of leaders have these common characteristics: [141]

- The ability to readily see potential in a person
- Tolerance of mistakes, brashness, and abrasiveness in order to see the potential develop
- Flexibility in responding to people
- Patience—knowing that time and experience are needed for development
- Perspective—the vision and ability to see down the road and to suggest next steps
- The ability to build up and encourage others

Mentors also:

- Give timely advice
- Recommend and suggest letters, articles, books, or other literature to offer perspective
- Provide financial support
- Offer freedom to emerge as a leader even beyond the level of the mentor

- Risk their own reputations in order to sponsor a mentee
- Model various aspects of leadership functions and challenge mentees to move towards them
- Direct mentees to needed resources that will further develop them
- Engage in shared leadership with mentees in order to increase their confidence, status and credibility.[142]

Remember, no one is indispensable, and we all must let go sooner or later. A leader's concentration must not be on the past or present, but the future. Organizations are reinvented with new generations of dreamers, and great leaders realize that success without a successor is failure.[143]

The balancing act is a struggle for leaders at every level, However, those that make an effort are much more productive leaders. To know when to lead, follow, or get out of the way, you must have balance. Stay balanced, my friends.

CHAPTER

7

A CALL TO ACTION

One of my mom's favorite songs was "A Charge to Keep I Have." I asked one day why that was one of her favorite songs, and I remember her answer vividly. She was enrolled at a local university in the sixties, obtaining her master's in education. One of her teachers was the local school superintendent, and he would often use the word "nigger" in class loosely, while she and others of the same hue sat there. They had two choices: to drop the class, which was needed for the completion of the program, or remain in the class and endure the barrage of racial slurs that were so vehemently used. In the sixties, it wouldn't have done much good to complain to department heads, because they were often of the same mindset. They chose to endure, and endure they did.

My mom said during those rough days, that song helped her survive—and some days, thrive—amid despair. She realized she was not only getting an advanced degree, she also had an obligation to pay it forward to the next generation of young Black educators and attorneys that would attend that school (which eventually included both of her sons). One day, I read this simple hymn written by Charles Wesley, to grasp the essence of the glue that held my mom and many like her together. It reads as follows:

A charge to keep I have,
A God to glorify,
A never dying soul to save,
And fit it for the sky,

To serve this present age,
My calling to fulfil,
Oh, may it all my power engage
To do my Master's will!

Arm me, with jealous care,
As in Thy sight to live;
And O Thy servant, Lord prepare
A strict account to give,

Help me to watch and pray,
And on Thyself rely,
Assured if I my trust betray
I shall forever die.

By the end of the second verse I was in tears, because I realized my mom and others like her were answering their call to action. A call is powerful thing, and it causes one to reach deep inside and do what sometimes seems like the impossible. As educational leaders, we have an ornate obligation to heed the call to action. Heeding the call may cause some of you to be ostracized, criticized, and in extreme cases, demoralized. However, I believe if you examine the lives of great leaders, you will see a trend of accomplishments often based on them heeding the call to action.

Booker T. Washington founded the Tuskegee Normal and Industrial Institute, known now as Tuskegee University because he heeded the call.

In 1895, W.E. B. Dubois became the First African American to earn a Ph.D. from Harvard University because he heeded the call.

Frederick Douglas became the first African American citizen in the nineteenth century to hold a high U.S. government rank because he heeded the call.

Geoffrey Canada founded the Harlem Children's Zone because he heeded the call.

Gillian Williams turned around a dismally failing school in New York and later founded School Turnaround because she heeded the call.

Will you heed the call to action? Will your name one day be remembered as someone who stood for principle as a principal?

Our profession is full of well-intended people doing ordinary things. Far too often we confuse movement or activity with progress. You can jog or run in place, which is movement, but not progress. Even though you are using energy, it's not progress! Are you moving forward? Are people following you?

"Progress" is the root word of "progression," which is to move gradually towards an advanced state. Hence, the philosophy of progressivism. American education has always struggled with a dual philosophy. One is essentialism, which espouses that students should only learn a certain set of prescribed material (meaning, don't think, just work). The other is progressivism, which espouses a curriculum that fosters critical thinking, creativity, and problem-solving. If you really want to make America great, adopt a progressive philosophy and create opportunities in your schools where students are challenged to think critically and solve problems.

I realize that the principalship is more than a notion, but I challenge you to rise to the level of greatness that our profession so desperately needs. If not you, then who? If not now, then when will someone heed the call to action?

ABOUT THE AUTHOR

Tyrone D. Burton, Ed.D., holds a bachelor's degree in Instrumental and Vocal Music Education from Northeast Louisiana State University, a master's degree in Educational Administration and Supervision from Louisiana State University, and a doctorate from Seton Hall University in Educational Leadership and Management Policy. He also received an honorary doctorate in Christian Counseling from Louisiana Baptist Theological Seminary.

After receiving his bachelor's degree, Dr. Burton taught band, choir, and elementary music in Caddo Parish at Mooringsport Elementary Fundamental School, where he was the first African American male teacher. He served as an Assistant Principal at Linear Middle School, where he successfully established a mentoring program to eliminate gang problems and lower the suspension rate. He later became an Assistant Principal at Donnie Bickham Middle School, where he instituted several programs to create an equitable learning environment for all students.

In August 2001, Dr. Burton became the Principal to Cherokee Park Elementary. At the time of his appointment, the school was in corrective action with an SPS of 44.4, and about to be taken over by the Department of Education. The

SPS increased ten points every year during Dr. Burton's first three years, thereby successfully losing the label of corrective action. During his principalship at Cherokee Park, he received the following awards, honors, and recognitions:

- Elementary Principal of the Year for Caddo Parish Schools (2013-2014)
- Top Gain School by the Louisiana State Department of Education (2012, 2013, 2014, 2016)
- $1.5M in grant awards (2001-2010)
- Cecil Picard Excellence in Education Award as a principal having achieved Value Added Score of five (2009-2010)
- National Presenter for the National Institute for Excellence in Teaching
- 2010 National Ambassadors Award from the National Institute for Excellence in Education
- Alliance for Education Award for student achievement and exemplary growth by the Louisiana Department of Education (2005, 2006, 2008, 2009, 2013, 2016)

Dr. Burton served on the superintendent's advisory committee and over his tenure, developed twenty-four educators that advanced to various positions within the local school board and the State Department of Education. He retired from Caddo Parish Schools in 2017 as a Distinguished Principal and was hired by the Rensselaerville

Institute, an educational think tank based in Albany, New York. He currently serves as a Turnaround Specialist. He is also the founder and CEO of Passion-Driven Leadership.

NOTES

1. Ruby Payne, *A Framework for Understanding Poverty* (Highlands: Aha! Process, 2001).

2. Ibid.

3. Dale Russakoff, *The Prize: Who's In Charge of America's Schools?* (New York: Houghton Mifflin Harcourt, 2015).

4. Ibid.

5. Alfino Flores, "Examining disparities in mathematics education: achievement gap or opportunity gap?" The High School Journal, 91(1), 29-42.

6. Russakoff, *The Prize, 91.*

7. Ibid.

8. Ibid.

9. Ibid.

10. Ibid.

11. Tom Rosentiel, "A Nation of 'Haves' and 'Have-Nots'? Far More Americans Now See Their Country as Sharply Divided Along Economic Lines," Pew Research Center, September 13, 2007.

12. Wilford Aikin, *The Story of the Eight-Year Study,* (New York: Harper, 1942).

13. William. J. Mathis, PhD, "The 'Common Core' Standards Initiative: An Effective Reform Tool?" Education and the Public Interest Center (EPIC) and the Education Policy Research Unit (EPRU), 2010. https://nepc.colorado.edu/sites/default/files/PB-NatStans-Mathis.pdf.

14. Ibid.

15. United States Department of Education, "No Child Left Behind: A New Era in Education" (PowerPoint presentation, April 24, 2006). https://www2.ed.gov/nclb/overview/intro/presentation/index.html.

16. Ibid.

17. Ibid.

18. William. J. Mathis, PhD, "The "Common Core" Standards Initiative: An Effective Reform Tool?" Education and the Public Interest Center (EPIC) and the Education Policy Research Unit (EPRU), 2010.

19. Christopher H. Tienken, "Common Core State Standards: An Example of Data-Less Decision Making," *AASA Journal of Scholarship and Practice* 7, no. 4 (Winter 2011), https://www.aasa.org/uploadedFiles/Publications/Newsletters/JSP_Winter2011.FINAL.pdf; Christopher H. Tienken and Yong Zhao, "Common Core National Standards: More Questions…and Answers," *AASA*

Journal of Scholarship and Practice 6, no. 4 (Winter 2010); Christopher H. Tienken and David Canton, "National Curriculum Standards: Let's Think It Over," *AASA Journal of Scholarship and Practice* 6, no. 3 (Fall 2009).

20. Organisation for Co-Operation and Economic Development, *Education at a Glance 2008 (*Paris: OECD Publications, 2008), Organisation for Co-Operation and Economic Development, *Top of the Class: High performers in Science in PISA 2006* (Paris: OECD Publications, 2009); United Nations, *Human Development Report 2010, The Real Wealth of Nations: Pathways to Human Development* (New York: MacMillan, 2010).

21. Vivek Wadhwa and Gary Gereffi, Framing the Engineering Outsourcing Debate (December 12, 2005). SSRN: https://ssrn.com/abstract=1015831 or http://dx.doi.org/10.2139/ssrn.1015831; Lindsay B. Lowell, Hal Salzman, and Hamutal Bernstein. "Steady as She Goes? Three Generations of Students through the Science and Engineering Pipeline" (paper presented at the annual meeting of the Association for Public Policy Management, Washington, D.C., November 7, 2009); Council on Competitiveness, *Competitiveness Index: Where America Stands* (Washington, D.C.: Council on Competitiveness, 2007); Klaus Schwab, *The Global Competitiveness Report 2010-2011* (Geneva: World

Economic Forum, 2010).

22. Keith Baker, "Are International Tests Worth Anything?" *Phi Delta Kappan* 89, no. 2 (October 2007): 101-104; Keith Baker, "A Bad Idea: National Standards Based on Test Scores, "*AASA Journal of Scholarship and Practice* 7, no. 3 (Fall 2010): 60-67; Francisco O. Ramirez, Xiaowei Luo, Evan Schofer, and John W. Meyer, "Student Achievement and National Economic Growth," *American Journal of Education* 113, no. 1 (November 2006): 1-29; Christopher H. Tienken, "Rankings of International Achievement Test Performance and Economic Strength: Correlation or Conjecture," *International Journal of Education Policy and Leadership* 3, no. 4: (April 2008): 1-15.

23. Frederick Harbison and Charles A. Myers, eds., *Education, Manpower, and Economic Growth: Strategies of Human Resource Development* (New York: McGraw Hill, 1956).

24. "College Enrollment and Work Activity for 2009 High School Graduates," United States Department of Labor, Bureau of Labor Statistics.

25. Organization for Co-Operation and Economic Development, *Top of the Class: High performers in Science in PISA 2006.*

26. U.S. Patent and Trademark Office 2010.

27. Ibid.

28. World Intellectual Property Organization (WIPO), *World Intellectual Property Indicators 2010*, (Geneva).

29. Schwab, *The Global Competitiveness Report 2010-2011*.

30. Neal McCluskey, "Behind the Curtain: Assessing the Case for National Standards," *Policy Analysis*, 661 (February 2010), http://www.cato.org/pubs/pas/pa661.pdf.

31. Tienken, "Common Core State Standards."

32. Hal Salzman and Lindsay Lowell, "Making the grade," Nature 483, (May 2008), p. 28-30. https://www.nature,com/articles/453028a?foxtrotcallback=true#citeas.

33. World Health Organization, *World Health Statistics 2010* (Geneva: WHO Press, 2010). https://www.who.int/whosis/whostat/EN_WHS10_Full.pdf?ua=1.

34. "The World Factbook," Central Intelligence Agency, https://www.cia.gov/library/publications/the-world-factbook/.

35. Heather Schwartz, *Housing Policy is School Policy: Economic Integrative Housing Promotes Academic Success in Montgomery County, Maryland*, (New York: The Century Foundation, 2010).

36. Margaret C. Wang, Geneva D. Haertel, and Herbert J. Walberg, "Toward a Knowledge Base for School

Learning," *Review of Educational Research* 63, no. 3 (September 1993): 249-294.

37. Ibid.

38. Thomas W. Tramaglini, "Transforming Curriculum: Establishing Curricular Democracy," July 27, 2005.

39. Douglas Reed, "Great (and Not so Great) Expectations: The Demographics of Proficiency Cut-Scores," *AASA Journal of Scholarship and Practice* 7, no. 3 (Fall 2010): 37-48.

40. Aikin, *The Story of the Eight-Year Study.*

41. Ellsworth Collings and William Heard Kilpatrick, *An Experiment with a Project Curriculum* (New York: Macmillan, 1923); Arthur T. Jersild, Robert L. Thorndike, Bernard Goldman, Jacob W. Wrightstone and John J. Loftus, "A Further Comparison of Pupils in 'Activity' and 'Non-Activity' Schools," *The Journal of Experimental Education* 9, no. 4 (June 1941); Robert L. Thorndike, "Mental Discipline in High School Studies," *Journal of Educational Psychology* 15, no. 1 (1924); Jacob W. Wrightstone, J. Rechetnick, W.A. McCall, and J.J. Loftus, "Measuring social performance factors in activity and control schools of New York City," *Teachers College Record* 40, no. 5 (1939); Jacob W. Wrightstone, "Appraisal of Experimental High School Practices," *Teachers College Record* 38, no. 3 (1936).

42. Lee Boleman and Terrance Deal, *The Four Frames of*

Education: Reframing Organizations, Artistry, Choice and Leadership (San Francisco: John Wiley & Sons, 1991).

43. Ronald A. Heifetz and Donald L. Laurie, "The Work of Leadership," Harvard Business Review, December 2001.

44. Stephen R. Covey, *The Seven Habits of Highly Effective People* (New York: Simon & Schuster, 1990).

45. Henry Stanley Haskins, *Meditations in Wall Street* (New York: William Morrow & Company, 1940).

46. Dr. Ernest T. Campbell, "Give Ye Them to Eat," *Sermons from Riverside* (1970): 8.

47. Martin Luther King, Jr., "I Have a Dream…" (March on Washington, Washington, D.C., August 28, 1963).

48. John Haltiwagner, "5 Quotes from Bill Gates That Prove You Need to Fail to Succeed," *The Elite Daily,* October 10, 2014.

49. Elena Aguilar, *The Art of Coaching Teams: Building Resilient Communities That Transform Schools* (San Francisco: Jossey-Bass, 2016).

50. Ibid.

51. Stephen R. Covey, *The Speed of Trust* (New York: Free Press, 2006).

52. Aguilar, *The Art of Coaching Teams: Building Resilient Communities That Transform Schools.*

53. Ibid.

54. Susan Dellinger, *Psycho-Geometrics: How to Use Geometric Psychology to Influence People,* Prentice Hall Direct, 1989.

55. David Kiersey and Marilyn Bates, *Please Understand Me: Character and Temperament Types* (Del Mar: Prometheus Nemesis Book Company, 1978).

56. Don Lowry, True Colors: Keys to Successful Teaching (Santa Ana, CA: True Colors, 1989).

57. Travis Bradberry and Jean Greaves, *Emotional Intelligence 2.0* (San Diego: TalentSmart, 2009).

58. Ibid.

59. Aguilar, *The Art of Coaching Teams: Building Resilient Communities That Transform Schools.*

60. Covey, *The Speed of Trust.*

61. Aguilar, *The Art of Coaching Teams: Building Resilient Communities That Transform Schools.*

62. Alexander Bogin and Phuong Nguyen-Hoang, "Property Left Behind: An Unintended Consequence of a No Child Left Behind 'Failing' School Designation," *Journal of Regional Science* 54, no. 5 (November 2014).

63. John C. Maxwell, *Developing the Leaders Around You: How to Help Others Reach Their Full Potential* (Nashville: Thomas Nelson Publishers, 1995).

64. Hans Finzel, *The Top Ten Mistakes Leaders Make* (Wheaton: Victor Books, 1994).

65. Wayne K. Hoy, "Academic Optimism: Pathway to Student Achievement [A 35-Year Academic Odyssey]," Seton Hall University, South Orange, NJ, 2010.

66. Steve Adubato, *You Are the Brand* (New Brunswick: Rutgers University Press, 2011).

67. Brian Backstrom, *School Turnaround Annotated Training Manual*, p. 68-69, https://rockinst.org/wp-content/uploads/2019/07/7-23-19-School-Turnaround-Efforts.pdf.

68. Aguilar, *The Art of Coaching Teams: Building Resilient Communities That Transform Schools.*

69. Finzel, *The Top Ten Mistakes Leaders Make.*

70. Hoy, "Academic Optimism," 2010.

71. Ibid.

72. Gary Gordon and Steve Crabtree. *Building Engaged Schools: Getting the Most Out of America's Classrooms* (New York: Gallup Press, 2006), 240.

73. Tyrone D. Burton, "A Case Study of the Implementation and Impact of the System for Teacher and Student Achievement (TAP)" (Ed.D. diss., Seton Hall University, 2017), 6.

74. Ibid., 44-45.

75. State and Local Implementation of the No Child Left Behind Act Volume VIII—Teacher Quality Under NCLB: Final Report, U.S. Department of Education's Office of

Planning, Evaluation, and Policy Development, 2009, xix.

76. Robert J. Marzano, Timothy Waters, and Brian A. McNulty, *School Leadership That Works: From Research to Results* (Alexandria: Association for Supervision and Curriculum Development, 2005).

77. William L. Sanders and June C. Rivers, *Cumulative and Residual Effects of Teachers on Future Student Academic Achievement* (Knoxville: University of Tennessee, 1996).

78. Covey, *The Seven Habits of Highly Effective People.*

79. Howard E. Gardner and Emma Laskin, *Leading Minds: An Anatomy Of Leadership* (New York: Basic Books, 1995); James M. Kouzes and Barry Z. Posner, *The Leadership Challenge: How to Keep Getting Extraordinary Things Done in Organizations* (San Francisco: Jossey-Bass, 1995); Elaine K. McEwan, *10 Traits of Highly Effective Principals: From Good to Great Performance* (Thousand Oaks: Corwin Press, 2003); John C. Maxwell, *The 21 Irrefutable Laws of Leadership: Follow Them and People Will Follow You* (Nashville: Thomas Nelson Publishers, 1998); Samuel G. Sava, *Proficiencies for Principals* (Alexandria: National Association of Elementary School Principals, 1997); Noel M. Tichy, *The Leadership Engine: How Winning Companies Build Leaders at Every Level* (New York: HarperCollins, 1997).

80. Richard F. Elmore, "Building a New Structure for School Leadership," Albert Shanker Institute (2000).

81. Burton, "A Case Study of the Implementation and Impact of the System for Teacher and Student Achievement (TAP)," 40.

82. Thomas J. Sergiovanni, *Moral Leadership: Getting to the Heart of School Improvement* (San Francisco: Jossey-Bass, 1992).

83. Elmore, "Building a New Structure for School Leadership."

84. Kathleen Cotton, *Principals and Student Achievement: What the Research Says* (Alexandria: Association for Supervision and Curriculum Development, 2003).

85. Marzano, Waters, and McNulty, *School Leadership That Works: From Research to Results.*

86. Cotton, *Principals and Student Achievement: What the Research Says.*

87. Marzano, Waters, and McNulty, *School Leadership That Works: From Research to Results.*

88. *Teacher Advancement Program (TAP) Handbook* (National Institute for Excellence in Teaching, 2006).

89. Michael Fullan, *Leading in a Culture of Change* (San Francisco: Josey-Bass, 2001).

90. McEwan, *10 Traits of Highly Effective Principals: From Good to Great Performance.*

91. James M. Kouzes and Barry Z. Posner, *The Five Practices*

of Exemplary Leadership (San Francisco: Josey-Bass, 2000).

92. *Teacher Advancement Program (TAP) Handbook.*

93. Kenneth A. Leithwood and Carolyn Riehl, "What We Know About Successful School Leadership," (Philadelphia: Temple University Press, 2003).

94. Mary Kay Stein and Laura D'Amico, "How Subjects Matter in School Leadership," paper presented at the annual meeting of the American Educational Research Association, New Orleans, January 2000.

95. Marzano, Waters, and McNulty, *School Leadership That Works: From Research to Results; Teacher Advancement Program (TAP) Handbook.*

96. Burton, "A Case Study of the Implementation and Impact of the System for Teacher and Student Achievement (TAP), 43.

97. Ibid., 37.

98. Ibid., 37-38.

99. Ibid., 38.

100. Ibid., 38.

101. Ibid., 39.

102. Ibid.

103. Ibid., 1.

104. Ibid., 13.

105. Ibid.

106. Ibid., 3.

107. Ibid.

108. Ibid.

109. Ibid.

110. Ibid., 2.

111. Bernard M. & Bruce J. Avolio, eds., *Improving Organizational Effectiveness Through Transformational Leadership* (Thousand Oaks, CA, Sage Publications, 1994).

112. Brian K. Cooper, James C. Sarros, and Joseph C. Santora, "Building a Climate for Innovation Through Transformational Leadership and Organizational Culture," *Journal of Leadership and Organizational Studies* 15, no. 2 (2008).

113. Cal P. Hauserman and Sheldon L. Stick, "The Leadership Teachers Want from Principals: Transformational," *Canadian Journal of Education* 36, no. 3 (2013): 184-203.

114. Hauserman and Stick, "The Leadership Teachers Want from Principals: Transformational," 184-203.

115. Ibid.

116. Bernard M. Bass, "Two Decades of Research and

Development in Transformational Leadership," *European Journal of Work and Organizational Psychology*, 8(1), 9-32, (1999).

117. Cooper, Sarros, and Santora, "Building a Climate for Innovation Through Transformational Leadership and Organizational Culture."

118. "What Is Transactional Leadership? How Structure Leads to Results," St. Thomas University, last modified May 8, 2018. https://online.stu.edu/articles/education/what-is-transactional-leadership.aspx.

119. St. Thomas University, "What Is Transactional Leadership? How Structure Leads to Results."

120. Dirk Van Dierendonck, "Servant Leadership: A Review and Synthesis," *Journal of Management* 37, no. 4 (2011), DOI: https://doi.org/10.1177/0149206310380462.

121. Robert K. Greenleaf, *Servant Leadership: A Journey into the Nature of Legitimate Power and Greatness* (Mahwah: Paulist Press, 1977).

122. Lucia Hamilton and Charlotte Knoche, "Modesty in Leadership: A Study of the Level Five Leader," *The International Journal of Servant-Leadership* 3, no. 1 (2007).

123. William Purkey and Betty Siegel, *Becoming an Invitational Leader: a New Approach to Professional and*

Personal Success, Humanix Books, Boca Raton Florida, October 10, 2002.

124. William Watson Purkey and John Michael Novak, *An Introduction to Invitational Theory: A Self-Concept Approach to Teaching, Learning, and Democratic Practice* (Belmont: Wadsworth Publishing, 2015).

125. Ibid.

126. James MacGregor Burns, *Leadership* (New York: Harper & Row, 1978).

127. Bernard M. Bass & Bruce J. Avolio, *Improving Organizational Effectiveness Through Transformational Leadership* (Thousand Oaks, CA: Sage Publications, 1994).

128. Holly Green, "Leadership: Then and Now," *Forbes,* August 30, 2011.

129. Ibid.

130. Kenneth Leithwood, Karen Seashore Louis, Stephen Anderson and Kyla Wahlstrom, "How Leadership Influences Student Learning" (Report), Center for Applied Research and Educational Improvement, September 2004.

131. Rose M. Ylimaki, *Critical Curriculum Leadership: A Framework for Progressive Education* (New York: Routledge, 2010).

132. "The Essential Guide to Evidence-Based Practice,"

Oxford Review, last modified 2020.

133. Hans Selye, *The Stress of Life* (New York: McGraw-Hill, 1956).

134. Dan Buettner, *The Blue Zones: Lessons for Living Longer From the People Who've Lived the Longest* (Washington, D.C.: National Geographic Society, 2008); Gary E. Fraser, *Diet, Life Expectancy and Chronic Disease: Studies of Seventh-Day Adventists and Other Vegetarians* (New York: Oxford University Press, 2003).

135. Covey, *The Speed of Trust.*

136. Covey, *The Seven Habits of Highly Effective People.*

137. Ibid.

138. Hans Finzel, *The Top Ten Mistakes Leaders Make.* Published by David C. Cook. Colorado Springs, CO. October 1, 2007.

139. Finzel, *The Top Ten Mistakes Leaders Make.* p. 178.

140. Ibid.

141. Paul D. Stanley, J. Robert Clinton. *Connecting: The Mentoring Relationships You Need to Succeed in Life.* (Colorado Spring: NavPress, 1992).

142. Ibid, p.188-189.

143. Ibid, p. 178, 199.

CPSIA information can be obtained
at www.ICGtesting.com
Printed in the USA
LVHW021319270321
682676LV00001B/59